PORTERS

SEASONAL
CELEBRATIONS
COOKBOOK

A CULINARY HISTORY OF FEASTS, FAIRS
AND FESTIVALS, WITH A TEMPTING COLLECTION
OF TRADITIONAL AND CONTEMPORARY RECIPES

Richard, Earl of Bradford,
and Carol Wilson

With love and thanks to my husband, Gordon, and my son,
Ivan, who patiently tested the recipes and offered their comments
and helpful advice.

Carol Wilson

First published in Great Britain in 2007 by
JR Books, 10 Greenland Street, London NW1 0ND
www.jrbooks.com

A catalogue record for this book is available from the British Library.

ISBN 978-1-906217-09-9

1 3 5 7 9 10 8 6 4 2

Printed by the MPG Books Group, Bodmin, Cornwall.

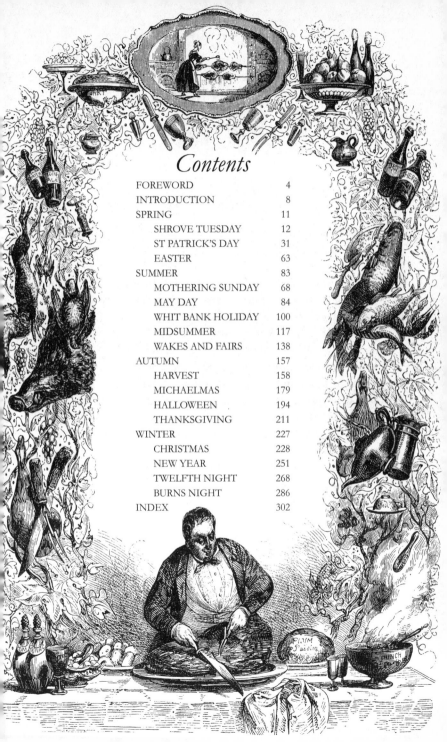

Contents

FOREWORD   4
INTRODUCTION   8
SPRING   11
   SHROVE TUESDAY   12
   ST PATRICK'S DAY   31
   EASTER   63
SUMMER   83
   MOTHERING SUNDAY   68
   MAY DAY   84
   WHIT BANK HOLIDAY   100
   MIDSUMMER   117
   WAKES AND FAIRS   138
AUTUMN   157
   HARVEST   158
   MICHAELMAS   179
   HALLOWEEN   194
   THANKSGIVING   211
WINTER   227
   CHRISTMAS   228
   NEW YEAR   251
   TWELFTH NIGHT   268
   BURNS NIGHT   286
INDEX   302

Foreword

Porters English Restaurant, which was created and opened by me in London in 1979, might be described as a bastion of reasonably priced English cooking in Covent Garden. The area was made famous by *My Fair Lady*, a film that took a young girl of humble origins and turned her into a lady – a transformation only slightly less difficult than the task that I took on.

However, 28 years later, it must be judged a fair success, and it has built quite a following of regular clients, many of whom have been coming there right from the start, and they are British in the main. This is something that must come as a bit of a surprise to many of the guidebook writers, who consistently describe it as a 'tourist restaurant'. Presumably they feel that our native cuisine can only possibly appeal to those from abroad: a strange and inaccurate assumption. Despite the fact that it does draw in a decent number of visitors to these shores, the reality is that the majority of our trade is home-grown.

Though we run a special pie every month, the menu doesn't alter all that frequently, mainly because all the dishes on it retain a fair bit of popularity – something that I have always felt is important, because something that nobody orders does not actually add to choice. Hence the fact that celebrations, particularly over the Christmas period, are important to Porters, as it gives us a chance to ring the changes.

So, Shrove Tuesday means that we can serve pancakes, either traditionally with sugar and lemon, or jazzed up a bit with the many options you can find in this book, while Halloween provides an opportunity for staff members to let their imagination run riot as they put on make-up and try to ensure that they look as hideous as possible. In December, with the restaurant festooned with decorations, we have to go for roast turkey with all the trimmings, followed of course by Christmas pudding and mince pies, with crackers for people to pull – mainly so that they can wear their silly hats throughout the meal to fit with the mood.

Despite the Englishness of Porters, it is surprising how many choose it as their preferred venue to mark Burns Night, St Patrick's Day and even Thanksgiving, but then maybe its informality and style of food suits those occasions when most people just want to let their hair down and have fun.

Where did the inspiration for Porters come from? It was certainly viewed by many as a brave step to start something so British and with hearty portions, especially at a time when the culinary fashion was for so-called French *nouvelle cuisine*: a succession of dainty, prettily presented dishes, but of a size that left you feeling somewhat less than satisfied. (We are still operating successfully, and where is *nouvelle cuisine* now? Fortunately consigned to the dustbin of gastronomic history.)

The answer, however, lies in my upbringing at our glorious ancestral family home, Weston Park in Shropshire, and also in the fact that my parents both enjoyed eating well. The staff in the kitchens would have been bored to tears if they hadn't had a chance to show their paces in the production of interesting meals. Moreover, the nationality of the cooks tended to vary, from Irish to Filipino, therefore the diversity of the dishes was quite considerable.

My mother, a genuinely gifted cook, seldom gave free rein to her talents in that direction, but, naturally creative, she tended to direct and orchestrate instead, ensuring that the talents of the chef at the time were employed to full effect. The result was the compilation of files of favourite recipes, so that the next person in charge of the kitchen could turn out those dishes that had previously been judged to be successes. Many of these have been used in this book.

The house in those days was very much the focal point of the village; indeed, the mansion and the park provided the employment for many of the locals, either inside as domestic staff or in keeping the fabric up to scratch, or outside in the gardens. When my father died in 1981 there were still eight gardeners, working either in the kitchen gardens or in the ornamental grounds and woodland walks surrounding the mansion. And then of course more people laboured on the farm and in the forestry department.

To a child, it was a wonderful, romantic paradise that was largely taken for granted simply because it was considered the normal way to live in a great house. It was rather like having your own personal playground. I remember when there were still shire-horses working in the fields, and, instead of using an efficient giant combine harvester, the corn was cut in the traditional way and collected in stooks, before being loaded up and hauled to the top end of the farmyard, where the gigantic wooden threshing machine, which heaved and shuddered as it worked to separate the wheat or barley, stood as a commanding presence. Then there was what I always referred to as the 'mangold mangling machine'. My favourite task was chucking the whole beet in at one end, watching it turning round and round and eventually come out as small chips to be fed to the sheep or cattle.

I suppose it was only natural that, growing up in the splendour of Weston Park, celebrations were an important feature of our lives. Every year, on Christmas Day, all the people in the village and nearby area that worked for the family would gather in the drawing room at Weston, and then, once we had joined them, the doors would open and, to the sound of Christmas carols, we would all go through to the library. Obviously we children always approached Christmas Day with a keen sense of anticipation; however, we were not allowed to open our presents until after this rather touching annual event. It was as if we desperately needed a drink but were being kept away from the oasis until after everyone else had slaked their thirst. First, we had to give out gifts to everyone from the village, even though we could see our own individual piles, each one allocated to a chair, before we were finally allowed to start opening ours. (All of this had been preceded by a very traditional family Christmas, beginning with the obligatory stockings, always with a lump of coal and a tangerine at end of the foot; then we had to get dressed and go off to church.)

Lunch was a fine affair – a huge turkey with different stuffings and all the trimmings – but even then we had to wait for it. Father would sharpen the knife and then carve with great expertise and style; gradually the plates filled with roast potatoes and Brussels sprouts, bread sauce, gravy, little chipolata sausages and rolled bacon, until eventually, tummies rumbling, we were allowed to begin eating.

There followed a brief hiatus while the attempts to light the brandy on the Christmas pudding failed (the simple secret is to heat the brandy in a pan first; never pour it straight from the bottle), and finally, accompanied by the smell of burned holly, in it came. It was served with homemade brandy butter, and of course the wonderful extra-thick Jersey cream from the farm. With luck, one of us might find a threepenny bit – the coin hidden inside the pudding. It may not sound much now, but it was amazing what it could buy then.

Then we would repair to the schoolroom, just in time to watch the Queen's Christmas message on television before allowing the lunch to digest. Before too long, however, we were faced with the reality of Christmas tea: another gargantuan feast, but mainly an excuse for the kitchen to show off its expertise in producing the Christmas cake and mince pies. Most important in my view was the chocolate log that only ever appeared on that day – just the richest, most chocolatey confection, with the thickest icing that you could ever imagine, disgustingly calorific but quite special and delicious. Finally, after all the present-giving and -receiving, we would retire upstairs again (we actually lived on the uppermost of three floors) where those who had room left for it were faced by cold turkey for supper. The next few days then became a battle of ingenuity for the kitchen, guided by my mother, to find different ways to use everything up. If I am to be honest, one time facing cold turkey is quite enough for me. I have never considered it to be the most interesting of meats, even when hot, and certainly far less so after it has cooled down and consequently dried out.

There were other festivals that loomed large in the Bradford family calendar and special dishes that we associated with them. However, those will be dealt with appropriately in the relevant part of this book.

Richard, Earl of Bradford

Introduction

The enjoyment of special food and drink has been associated with celebrations and festivals since ancient times and has always added to the importance of the occasion. People have gathered around a table to eat and drink to observe special occasions since time immemorial.

Our ancestors regarded foods for high days and holidays (both religious and secular) as very special. The majority of people knew that, after the holiday, their diet would return to the usual plain, simple, even frugal fare. Seasonal foods therefore were eagerly anticipated for their specific flavours: rich and spicy in winter, light and fresh in spring and summer, and earthy and hearty in the autumn.

Some festive foods have become an inextricable part of many festivals, and British cuisine is no exception. Here we have pancakes on Shrove Tuesday for instance, simnel cake at Easter, gingerbread at Halloween and plum pudding at Christmas. The recipes and traditions associated with these and other specialities date from a time when people took time over food made with love and care and enjoyed the taste of good wholesome ingredients.

Such recipes have managed to survive throughout the centuries, frequently undergoing intervention and adaptation, incorporating modern ideas as culinary traditions and tastes have changed – adding a little of this or a pinch of that or using whatever happened to be available to meet the tastes of a particular time. There's a certain pleasure in making the same tempting dishes that our grandmothers and their grandmothers before them cooked for friends and family, incorporating our own little touches along the way. Over time, these recipes have been reworked, renewed and revitalized, with new life breathed into them. This is important, because such recipes have gradually evolved through the years to become a much-loved and treasured part of our heritage, both at home and when dining out.

Spring

SHROVE TUESDAY

Shrove Tuesday (the day before Ash Wednesday, the start of Lent) is, in the UK and much of Europe, the traditional day for enjoying pancakes. Originally it was intended to use up stocks of milk, butter and eggs, which were forbidden during Lent. In some parts of northern England and Scotland, the day is also known as 'Fastern's' or 'Fassern's Eve', because it is the day before the start of the Lenten fast. The word 'carnival' is said to be derived from the Latin *carne vale*, meaning literally a 'farewell to meat'. Whatever its origins, Shrove Tuesday also became a day for pranks, games, gambling, football, archery and feasting. Well-to-do households also included plays and masques in the revelries.

The custom of eating pancakes dates back to the fifteenth century, and tossing pancakes can be traced to the time of Elizabeth I. Early pancakes made with flour, eggs, milk and sometimes ground spices were thick and soft, but by the eighteenth century they had became thin and crisp.

Many customs and superstitions are also associated with pancakes. One was 'Shroving' or 'Lent Crocking', when children went from house to house asking for pancakes, often in rhyme. This custom developed from earlier days, when poor villagers had the right to beg for pancakes on this day, but if no pancakes were forthcoming, they threatened to throw broken crockery at the door!

In the British Midlands, the first pancake was given to the chickens to ensure their fertility during the year. Similarly, some regions believed that the first three pancakes to be cooked were sacred, and these were each marked with a cross before being sprinkled with salt to ward off evil and then set aside. In the north of England, pancake parties were held each year on Shrove Tuesday until the 1940s.

Irish girls were given the afternoon off school to make their pancake batter and cook pancakes in the evening. Traditionally the eldest unmarried daughter tossed the first pancake; if she did so successfully, it meant that she would be married within the year. Irish housewives were fond of playing tricks on new young wives by sending them off to find a fictional 'pancake sieve'.

Shrove Tuesday was a day when 'nobody should be without meat', and every Irish family, no matter how poor, sat down to eat a piece of bacon at the very least. The Scots, meanwhile, preferred beef, particularly beef broth on Shrove Tuesday to ensure prosperity for the coming year.

In the Scottish Highlands, special oatcakes known as bannocks as well as *bannich junit*, or 'sauty' bannocks, were made using eggs and oatmeal mixed with salt to make them 'sauty' before being baked or cooked on a 'girdle', or griddle. A charm was inserted into the dough before cooking; an unmarried person who found the charm was sure to be married during the next year. There were also Scotch pancakes or drop scones: small, thick pancakes baked on a griddle, a method of cooking that predates oven-baking.

In Wales, meanwhile, poor people went from door to door begging for flour and lard or butter to make *crempog:* the Welsh word for 'pancake'. In some parts of Wales children kicked tin cans up and down the streets, possibly to commemorate the putting away of cooking utensils and pans used to cook meat and other banned foods during Lent.

America, of course, celebrates Shrove Tuesday as Mardi Gras, ('Fat Tuesday'), which is said to takes its name from the custom of parading a fat ox through the streets of Paris on this day. It's a time for fun and carnivals, with bands and colourful parades, especially in New Orleans, Louisiana, where there is a long French tradition and where the first Mardi Gras carnival took place in 1827. The New Orleans celebrations are now world-famous.

King cake is an essential part of the New Orleans celebrations and a plastic toy baby is concealed inside. The person who finds the baby is obliged to buy or make another king cake or hold a party. The cake is actually a sweet, rich bread topped with a sweet glaze and sprinkled with coloured sugar – purple (for justice), green (for faith) and gold (for power). Thousands of the delicious cakes are sold at Mardi Gras and are also sent all over the world for homesick Americans to enjoy on Mardi Gras.

Pancake breakfasts are popular fundraising events in the USA, where a wide variety of pancakes are served with different toppings and fillings. Although in England it is traditional to serve pancakes sprinkled with lemon juice and sugar, they can also be delicious when filled with stewed fresh fruit, or spread with jam, preserves or chocolate and served with fresh whipped cream or ice cream for a quick dessert. Savoury pancake fillings make a satisfying meal, served with a green salad or other vegetables.

Basic pancake recipe

Makes 10-12 18-20cm/7-8-inch pancakes

115g/4oz plain (all-purpose) flour
Pinch of salt
1 egg
300ml/1¼ cups milk
1 teaspoon oil or melted butter
Oil for cooking

Sift the dry ingredients into a mixing bowl and make a well in the centre. Add the egg and beat well. Add half the milk and oil and beat until smooth. Stir in the rest of the milk.

Lightly oil a pancake pan or frying pan and heat until smoking-hot. Add enough batter for a thin, even coating. Cook until set and lightlygolden, then turn over and cook for another 30 seconds. Remove from the pan and repeat with the remaining batter, greasing the pan between each pancake.

VARIATIONS TO THE BASIC PANCAKE BATTER
Stir 2 tablespoons sugar and 2-3 tablespoons chopped chocolate (milk or plain/dark) into the batter before cooking.

Add 2 tablespoons sugar, 1 teaspoon ground cinnamon and 50g/2 ounces finely chopped walnuts or sultanas (white raisins) to the batter before cooking.

Thicker pancakes will need a minute or two longer cooking time. Adding a little oil or melted butter to the batter keeps the pancakes moist and prevents them from becoming rubbery. Make sure the pan is very hot before you add the batter.

Keep pancakes warm by layering a sheet of greaseproof (waxed) paper between each. Cover with a piece of buttered greaseproof or foil and place in a low oven, 150°C/300°F/gas mark 2.

Seafood pancakes
(Bradford Family Recipe)

<u>For the filling</u>
50g/½ stick butter
4 tablespoons finely chopped onion
2 slices raw veal or ham, finely chopped
2 tablespoons plain (all-purpose) flour
Salt and pepper
¼ teaspoon freshly grated nutmeg
¼ teaspoon cayenne pepper
1 bay leaf, crushed
2 tablespoons chopped parsley
600ml/2½ cups milk, warmed
2 egg yolks, beaten
2 tablespoons double (heavy) cream
2 tablespoons lemon juice
4-6 tablespoons dry white wine
4 tablespoons freshly grated Parmesan cheese
450g/1 pound freshly cooked lobster, crab or mussels – or a combination of all three

10 pancakes

Butter a large baking dish. Melt the butter in a sauté pan and gently cook the onions until soft and transparent.

Add the veal or ham and continue to cook stirring for 2-3 minutes. Sprinkle with the flour and cook stirring for 2 minutes. Season to taste with salt and pepper and add the nutmeg and cayenne.

Stir in the bay leaf and parsley and gradually add the warm milk until well blended.

Whisk the egg yolks, cream, lemon juice and wine in a bowl until blended. Strain the sauce into the bowl and stir well.

Tip everything into a pan and cook over a very low heat until thickened. Do not allow to become too hot or boil or the mixture will curdle.

Preheat the grill (broiler).

Stir in half the grated cheese and all the shellfish and heat through gently. Spoon about 2 tablespoons of the seafood filling on each pancake and roll up loosely.

Place the pancakes in a buttered baking dish and pour over the remaining sauce. Sprinkle with the remaining cheese and put under the hot grill until brown and bubbling.

All the family – with the exception of my sister Caroline, who was put off by her experience of very poor-quality fish at school – adored seafood pancakes, particularly when they contained plenty of lobster. It felt like a touch of luxury in something that appeared so normal otherwise; when you look at the completed dish, almost anything could be hiding inside the pancakes. However, it could be guaranteed that the platter never went back anything other than empty. RB

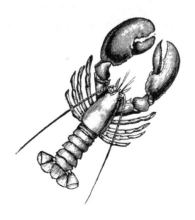

Chicken and mushroom pancakes

For the filling
50g/½ stick butter
115g/4 ounces mushrooms, sliced or chopped
1 small onion, finely chopped
50g/2 ounces plain (all-purpose) flour
300ml/1¼ cups chicken stock
50ml/¼ cup dry white wine
450g/1 pound cooked chicken, sliced or chopped
2 tablespoons double (heavy) cream
Salt and pepper to taste

8 pancakes

Preheat the oven to 200°C/400°F/gas mark 6. Grease a large baking dish.

Melt half the butter in a frying pan and fry the mushrooms and onion until soft.

Add the remaining butter, stir in the flour and cook for 1 minute. Add the stock and wine and stir until boiling. Simmer gently for 2-3 minutes.

Remove from the heat and stir in the chicken and cream. Season to taste with salt and pepper. Spoon some of the filling onto each pancake and roll up.

Arrange the stuffed pancakes in the baking dish. Cover closely with buttered foil and bake in the oven for 15-20 minutes until heated through.

Not all that long ago, chicken was a luxury, a treat to be anticipated on special occasions. The best-flavoured meat comes from an organic or free-range bird, which has been allowed to roam outdoors and feed on grain.

St Clement's pancakes

<u>*For the filling*</u>
115g/1 stick butter
75g/3 ounces sugar
Grated zest and juice of 1 orange
Grated zest and juice of ½ lemon
2 tablespoons orange liqueur
2 tablespoons lemon liqueur
Sugar for sprinkling

10 thin pancakes

Preheat the oven to 200°C/400°F/gas mark 6.

Cream the butter and sugar until soft, then stir in the grated zests. Beat in almost all the liqueurs, adding them very slowly, a little at a time, then gradually beat in the juices.

Spread the mixture evenly over half of each pancake. Fold each pancake in half, then in quarters and lay them overlapping in a well-buttered dish.

Sprinkle heavily with sugar and heat through in the oven for 5-8 minutes. Remove from the oven and sprinkle with the remaining liqueurs and serve hot.

To freeze: wrap the cold, filled, folded pancakes in non-stick paper and thick foil. To reheat: unwrap and place the pancakes in a well-buttered dish and follow the recipe instructions as above, but cook for 7-10 minutes.

These refreshing citrus pancakes make a very elegant dessert that can be ready in just a few minutes, even if cooked straight from the freezer.

Black cherry pancakes with kirsch sauce

For the filling and sauce
1 x 425g/15-ounce can black cherries in syrup, stones removed
175g/6 ounces full-fat cream cheese
75g/3 ounces golden caster (golden superfine or baker's) sugar
1 teaspoon grated lemon zest
2 tablespoons cornflour (cornstarch)
4 tablespoons kirsch

8 pancakes

Drain the cherries, reserving the syrup and set aside a quarter of the cherries for the sauce.

Beat the cheese, sugar and grated zest together until soft and fluffy. Chop the remaining cherries roughly and fold them into the cheese mixture.

Spread a little cherry mixture on each pancake and fold into triangles. Arrange in a serving dish and keep warm.

Blend the cornflour (cornstarch) and kirsch together until smooth. Add the reserved cherries and syrup. Heat until boiling, stirring, then reduce the heat and simmer for a minute or two until thickened.

Spoon the cherry sauce over the pancakes and serve immediately.

This makes a sophisticated dessert and is ideal for entertaining. It's especially delicious served with vanilla or cherry ice cream.

Chocolate nut pancake stack

<u>*For the filling*</u>
115g/4 ounces plain (dark) chocolate, finely chopped or grated
115g/4 ounces walnuts or hazelnuts, chopped
115g/4 ounces light muscovado (soft light brown) sugar
75g/3 ounces sultanas (white raisins)
Grated zest 1 small orange
25g/¼ stick butter

6 pancakes

Preheat the oven to 180°C/350°F/gas mark 4. Butter a large baking dish.

Combine all the filling ingredients except the butter and spread evenly over each pancake. Stack in the baking dish, finishing with a plain pancake. Dot with butter and cook for 10-15 minutes.

Cut into wedges like a cake. Serve with whipped cream or ice cream.

A scrumptiously indulgent dessert that's delicious after a light main course.

Pancake gateau

For the filling and sauce
4 egg yolks
50g/2 ounces sugar
225ml/1 cup double (heavy) or whipping cream
½ teaspoon vanilla extract
300ml/1¼ cups apricot or apple purée

8 thin pancakes

Preheat the oven to 180°C/350°F/gas mark 4. Butter a deep baking or soufflé dish.

Whisk the egg yolks and sugar until very light. Whisk in the cream and vanilla and continue whisking until thick.

Layer the pancakes and fruit purée in the dish, ending with a pancake. Pour the custard mixture over, ensuring it goes down the sides.

Bake for 20-30 minutes. Cool in the dish and cut into wedges to serve.

Pancakes layered with fruit purée and creamy custard, then baked until golden and bubbling, make a delicious dessert.

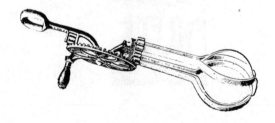

Potato flour pancakes

Wheat- and gluten-free

6 eggs
175g/6 ounces potato flour
Pinch of salt
330ml/1⅓ cups water, approximately
Oil for cooking

Beat the eggs until frothy and gradually whisk in the potato flour, salt and water until the mixture is pale yellow and foamy. Cover and leave to stand for 30 minutes.

Beat the batter again before cooking.

Heat a little oil in a frying pan and when very hot pour in sufficient batter to cover the base of the pan. Cook for a few minutes on each side until crisp and golden.

Serve with lemon and sugar, honey or maple syrup.

These crisp, light pancakes are ideal for anyone who can't tolerate wheat or gluten.

Coconut pancakes

Wheat- and gluten-free

600ml/2½ cups coconut milk (available in cans from supermarkets and
 ethnic food stores)
3 eggs, beaten
150g/5½ ounces rice flour
115g/4 ounces desiccated
 (shredded) coconut
1 tablespoon sugar
Sugar and lemon juice, to finish

Put all the ingredients into
a mixing bowl and beat well to
form a smooth batter.

Pour a thin stream of batter into a hot greased
frying pan so that the batter flows thinly across the surface.
Cook until set, then turn over to cook the other side.

Sprinkle with sugar and lemon juice to serve

*These deliciously light pancakes are ideal for anyone with an intolerance to
wheat or suffering from coeliac disease.*

Soufflé saucer pancakes

50g/½ stick butter
50g/2 ounces sugar
2 eggs
50g/2 ounces self-raising (self-rising) flour
300ml/1¼ cups milk
Jam or preserves, and extra sugar to serve

Preheat the oven to 190°C/375°F/gas mark 5. Grease 8 saucers and put them into the oven to heat.

Cream the butter and sugar until soft and light. Beat in the eggs, one at a time, adding a little of the flour each time. Beat in the rest of the flour.

Heat the milk until hot, but not boiling and pour into the flour mixture, beating well.

Pour the mixture into the hot saucers and bake for 15-20 minutes until puffy and golden. Put a spoonful of jam or preserves on each pancake and fold in half. Sprinkle with sugar and serve at once.

These unusual pancakes are cooked in the oven on greased saucers and will puff up like soufflés during cooking.

Gloucestershire suet pancakes

6 tablespoons suet or chilled butter, diced
175g/6 ounces plain (all-purpose) flour
1 teaspoon baking powder
Pinch of salt
2 eggs
2-3 tablespoons milk
Oil for frying

Rub the fat into the flour, baking powder and salt, until the mixture resembles breadcrumbs.

Beat the eggs with the milk, stir into the flour mixture and mix to a stiff dough.

Roll out the dough on a floured board to a thickness of about 5mm/¼ inch and cut into 10 rounds.

Heat the oil in a frying pan and fry the pancakes, turning once during cooking, until golden brown on both sides. Serve immediately.

These are quite different to ordinary pancakes and have a grainier texture. They're delicious with sausages, eggs and bacon or a sweet filling.

Scotch pancakes with bananas and toffee sauce

225g/8 ounces self-raising (self-rising) flour
50g/2 ounces caster sugar
2 eggs
300ml/1¼ cups milk
1 teaspoon cream of tartar
3 large, firm bananas

For the toffee sauce
115g/1 stick unsalted butter
115g/4 ounces light muscovado (soft light brown) sugar
150ml/⅝ cup double (heavy) cream
½ teaspoon vanilla extract

Sift the flour into a mixing bowl and stir in the sugar. Add the eggs, milk and cream of tartar and beat well to a thick batter.

Beat a greased griddle or heavy-based frying pan and pour on a tablespoon of batter. Cook over a medium heat until bubbles form on the surface. Gently turn the pancake over and cook the other side until golden. Wrap the cooked pancakes in a clean tea towel (dishcloth) to keep them soft.

For the toffee sauce: put all the ingredients into a pan over a low heat and stir until the butter has melted and the sugar has dissolved. Bring to the boil and boil the sauce for about 3-4 minutes; as it boils the sauce will thicken.

Slice the bananas. Spread the pancakes with toffee sauce and stack them with sliced bananas in a pile, then pour on more sauce. Serve with ice cream or whipped cream.

These thick, soft pancakes are also known as 'drop scones' and are delicious spread with butter and jam or preserves.

Crempog

(Welsh Pancakes)

8 generous tablespoons plain (all-purpose) flour
Pinch of salt
½ teaspoon bicarbonate of soda (baking soda)
300ml / 1¼ cups buttermilk
1 large egg, beaten
Lard or butter for cooking

Sift the flour and salt into a mixing bowl.

Stir the bicarbonate of soda into the buttermilk.

Stir the milk mixture into the flour with the egg and beat
thoroughly for about 5 minutes, or until smooth.

Grease a griddle or heavy frying pan with a little butter. Drop
tablespoonfuls of the batter on the griddle and cook until golden
and set. Turn over and cook the other side.

Serve warm with butter, honey, jam or preserves.

In some parts of Wales these pancakes are known as ffroes *and are always
served fresh and hot, piled up with plenty of butter.*

Mardi Gras king cake

25g/1 ounce fresh yeast
90ml/scant ½ cup warm, creamy milk
450g/1 pound strong (bread) flour, plus extra
 for kneading
1 teaspoon salt
1 tablespoon sugar
1 teaspoon ground cinnamon
1 teaspoon finely grated lemon zest
4 eggs plus 1 egg yolk
200g/2 sticks unsalted butter, softened

For the glaze
115g/4 ounces icing (confectioner's) sugar
2-3 teaspoons warm water
¼ teaspoon vanilla extract

For the coloured sugars
Green, purple and yellow food colouring
6 tablespoons sugar

Dissolve the yeast in the milk, mixing lightly.

Put the flour, salt, sugar, cinnamon and lemon zest in a mixing
bowl and make a well in the centre. Pour in the yeast mixture, and
then break in the whole eggs. Mix very well together and gradually
beat in the butter, a little at a time until a soft dough forms, then
knead in the bowl for 5 minutes.

Turn out and knead for 10 minutes until shiny and elastic – you
may need a little more flour. Place the dough into a well-buttered
bowl, turning it until well coated with butter. Cover the bowl and
put in a warm place for about 1 hour 30 minutes, or until doubled
in size.

Punch down the risen dough with your fists and knead for a few minutes. Shape the dough into a sausage shape and pinch the ends together to seal and form a circle. Place the dough on a buttered baking tray and cover with a tea towel (dishcloth). Leave to rise in a warm place for 45 minutes, until doubled in volume.

Preheat the oven to 190°C/375F/gas mark 5.

Beat the egg yolk with 1 teaspoon water and brush over the dough. Bake for about 25-35 minutes until golden brown. Cool.

For the glaze: sift the icing sugar into a bowl and stir in the water and vanilla until smooth and thick. Drizzle over the cold cake.

For the coloured sugars: put 2 tablespoons sugar in each of 3 small bowls. Add a tiny amount of colouring to each bowl and mix well. Sprinkle over the icing before it sets.

Innovative New Orleans bakers have developed numerous shapes and sizes of king cake. Modern flavours include chocolate, blueberry, cream cheese, lemon and pecan praline.

ST PATRICK'S DAY

The feast of St Patrick, Ireland's much-loved patron saint, is celebrated on March 17th with festivals and parades, not only in Ireland but throughout the world by Irish people and those of Irish descent. In Dublin, Ireland's capital, St Patrick's Festival is an enormously popular annual event and lasts for several days, with music, theatre, concerts, fireworks, carnivals and dancing. Traditionally, Irish people wear shamrocks in their lapels on St Patrick's Day, while in the past girls wore green ribbons in their hair – and indeed, some still do so.

St Patrick was born in Britain towards the end of the fourth century. He was taken prisoner by Irish raiders when he was 16 and transported to Ireland, where he remained a prisoner for six years. Patrick escaped back to Britain, where he trained as a priest; after his ordination he returned to Ireland as a missionary. For 40 years, he travelled to the remotest parts of Ireland, baptizing large numbers of people, ordaining clergy, founding monasteries and performing many miracles. He died and was buried at Down, in Ulster. The exact burial spot is not clear, but in 1900 a memorial stone made from a slab of granite from the Mourne Mountains was erected to mark what is believed to be his grave, which today lies in the graveyard of Down Cathedral, built in 1183.

Interestingly, the very first St Patrick's Day Parade took place in New York in 1762, when Irish soldiers marched through the city accompanied by Irish music. The parade has continued uninterrupted every year since then and starts on 44th Street and

Fifth Avenue, then travels east on 86th Street to Third Avenue. Traditionally the New York archbishop reviews the parade in front of St Patrick's Cathedral.

The New York City St Patrick's Day Parade is the longest-running civilian parade in the world. Almost three million people turn out to watch the spectacular event, which takes place entirely on foot – no cars or other vehicles are allowed. Over 150,000 people march up Fifth Avenue, led by members of the 165th Infantry (originally the Irish 69th Regiment), and the parade is sponsored by the Ancient Order of Hibernians. The marchers include members of various Irish societies from New York and around the country, as well as some from overseas. Large delegations include the Emerald Societies of the New York City Police and Fire departments, and politicians standing for office within a 50-mile radius.

Chicago, along with other American cities, also has a parade but is uniquely famous for dyeing the Chicago River green on St Patrick's Day! The tradition began in 1962, when a pipe-fitters' union, with the permission of the mayor, poured 45 kilograms (99 pounds) of green vegetable dye into the river. Today only 18 kilos (around 40 pounds) of dye are used – just enough to turn the river a perfect shade of emerald green for several hours.

Since the 1990s, the Irish *taoisigh* (prime ministers) have attended special functions either on St Patrick's Day or a day or two earlier, in the White House, where they present shamrocks to the US president and the speaker of the house.

In Britain, a member of the Royal Family presents a shamrock specially flown over from Ireland to members of the Irish Guards, a regiment in the British Army made up of Irish people from both Northern Ireland and the Republic of Ireland.

In Ireland, St Patrick's Day is a national holiday, with family dinners and special foods playing an important role in the festivities. The feast day falls during Lent, but the Lenten ban on meat is waived to allow Irish families the traditional meal of bacon and cabbage. Time-honoured food and drink are essential to the celebrations, including Irish stout and whiskey.

Ireland has an enduring tradition of producing superb food, and boasts a wonderful heritage of delicious, long-established recipes. There's far more to Irish food than Irish stew: first-rate salmon and other fish from Ireland's unpolluted rivers and lakes; rich dairy products; a vast choice of potato dishes; magnificent home baking; and of course, renowned Irish specialities such as Dublin coddle and soda bread.

Oysters with bacon

8-10 fresh oysters, shucked and shells reserved and cleaned
Lemon juice
4-5 thin rashers of streaky bacon

Preheat the grill (broiler).

Put a few drops of lemon juice on each oyster. Cut each bacon rasher in half and wrap around each oyster. Secure each with a cocktail stick.

Cook under a moderate heat for 5 minutes, turning once. Return each oyster to the shell and serve immediately.

Ireland is renowned for the quality and flavour of its native oysters. They're enjoyed raw from the shell, washed down with a glass of Irish stout, or baked with bacon. Open by holding the oyster in one hand, well wrapped in a tea towel (dishcloth). Push the point of an oyster knife (or other strong knife) into the oyster's hinge and apply pressure to open, ensuring that the liquor is retained. Alternatively, ask your fishmonger to do this. Serve on a plate of crushed ice with lemon wedges and sip the liquor from the shell.

Citrus ginger salmon steaks

900g/2 pounds salmon steaks
½ teaspoon ground white pepper
½ teaspoon ground ginger
1 teaspoon salt
50ml/¼ cup orange juice
1 tablespoon lemon juice
1 tablespoon white-wine vinegar
50ml/¼ cup ginger wine (use ginger ale if unavailable)
4 teaspoons finely chopped fresh parsley
Finely grated zest of 1 orange
Finely grated zest of 1 lemon

Place the salmon steaks in a large, shallow frying pan. Mix the pepper, ginger, and salt with the orange and lemon juice, vinegar and wine and sprinkle over the fish. Cover and heat until simmering, then leave to simmer for 5 minutes.

Turn the salmon steaks over and add the parsley and orange and lemon zest. Cover the pan and simmer for another 5-10 minutes, until the fish is cooked through; the actual cooking time will depend on the thickness of the fish.

Serve the salmon with the pan juices, boiled new potatoes and green vegetables.

Salmon has graced the tables of Irish kings and nobles since antiquity, and Irish salmon is deservedly renowned for its outstanding quality, flavour and texture. This is not a traditional Irish recipe, but the clear, sharp flavours complement the rich yet delicate taste of the fish.

Salmon with sorrel

(Bradford Family Recipe)

4-6 salmon steaks
600ml/2½ cups fish or vegetable stock
1 tablespoon tomato purée (paste)
55g/½ stick butter
2 tablespoons flour
300ml/1¼ cups double (heavy) cream
Salt and pepper
25g/¼ stick butter, melted
Sorrel leaves, snipped

Put the salmon steaks in a frying pan and pour in the stock. Bring to the boil, cover and simmer gently for about 10 minutes until the salmon is cooked. Transfer the salmon to a plate and keep warm.

Add the tomato purée to the stock, bring to the boil and cook steadily until reduced by half.

Melt the butter in a pan and stir in the flour. Cook over a low heat to a paste but do not allow to brown. Add the cream, increase the heat and stir until the sauce thickens. Stir just enough of the reduced stock into the cream sauce to add colour and flavour. Season to taste with salt and pepper.

Stir the butter into the sorrel leaves, stir into the sauce and bring to the boil. Put the salmon steaks on serving plates and pour over the sauce. Serve immediately.

This was considered a special dish because all the salmon was wild in bygone days, and usually depended on my father or one of his local friends having returned successfully from a fishing trip to Scotland. Sorrel, which actually grows wild in most part of Britain, is sadly underused in cooking. RB

Dublin coddle

1 tablespoon oil
9 large pork sausages, cut into large chunks
9 thick slices bacon or gammon (ham), cut into large pieces
4 large onions, sliced
1 kg/2¼ pounds floury potatoes, peeled and sliced
Salt and pepper
700ml/3 cups boiling ham or vegetable stock
3 tablespoons finely chopped parsley

Heat the oil in a frying pan and quickly brown the sausages and bacon for a few minutes.

Drain off the fat and mix the sausages with the onions, bacon and potatoes and season with salt and pepper.

Place in a large pan and pour in the boiling stock. Cover tightly and simmer gently for 1-1½ hours, or until the liquid is very much reduced and the potatoes are soft but not mushy.

Sprinkle with parsley and serve at once with soda bread.

This was reputedly a favourite dish of Jonathan Swift and is also mentioned in several Irish literary references, including the works of the famous Irish writer and poet James Joyce. Dublin butchers sell 'bacon bits': offcuts from various types of bacon especially for making coddle.

Irish stew with stout

3 tablespoons oil
900g/2 pounds stewing lamb, cut into 4cm/1½-inch pieces
2 large onions, roughly chopped
6 carrots, roughly chopped
1 heaped tablespoon flour
Salt and pepper
450ml/2 cups Irish stout (or other dark beer)
150ml/⅝ cup beef stock
2 bay leaves
1 tablespoon molasses or black treacle, optional

Preheat the oven to 170°C/325°F/gas mark 3.

Heat the oil in an ovenproof casserole, add the meat and fry quickly in batches until brown on all sides. Remove the meat and add the chopped onions and carrots to the fat left in the pan and cook until lightly browned. Add the flour, salt and pepper and cook for 1 minute before adding the stout, beef stock, bay leaves and molasses to the pan.

Bring to the boil, stirring. Add the meat and cover the casserole. Transfer to the oven and cook for 2-3 hours, or until the meat is very tender but not stringy. Serve with boiled or mashed potatoes and cabbage.

Irish stew, or stobhach gaelach, *as it is called in Irish, is a hearty, filling dish that's traditionally made with lamb or mutton, although it can also be made with cubed stewing beef if you prefer. The molasses is optional but imparts a lovely rich flavour to the stew.*

Bacon, cabbage and potato bake

25g/¼ stick butter
1 tablespoon oil
150g/5½ ounces bacon, diced
250g/9 ounces green cabbage, shredded
1 large onion, sliced
1 clove garlic, optional
125ml/½ cup single (light) cream
125ml/½ cup milk
Salt and pepper
675g/1½ pounds potatoes, peeled and thinly sliced
115g/4 ounces mature Irish Cheddar or Dubliner cheese, grated

Preheat the oven to 180°C/350°F/gas mark 4.

Heat the butter and oil in a non-stick frying pan and cook the bacon until crisp and golden. Add the cabbage, onion and garlic and cook for a few minutes until the cabbage is just wilted.

Heat the cream and milk to boiling point, then immediately remove from the heat.

Layer the cabbage mixture with the potatoes and cheese in a greased 1-litre/1-quart baking dish, finishing with the potatoes. Sprinkle with the grated cheese and pour over the cream mixture. Bake for 40-45 minutes until bubbling hot and the potatoes are tender.

Bacon and cabbage is a traditional and much-loved Irish dish. This updated recipe bakes the customary ingredients with cream and is topped with cheese for a wonderfully tasty, satisfying main course.

Soda bread

225g/8 ounces plain (all-purpose) flour, plus extra for sprinkling
1 teaspoon bicarbonate of soda (baking soda)
1 teaspoon salt
½ teaspoon cream of tartar
25g/¼ stick butter
150ml/⅝ cup buttermilk

Preheat the oven to 200°C/400°F/gas mark 6.

Sift the dry ingredients into a large mixing bowl and rub in the
butter until well combined. Make a well in the centre and pour in
the buttermilk, mixing quickly with a broad-bladed knife, until the
mixture forms a dough.

Turn out onto a floured board and knead very lightly. Press or
roll the dough into a round about 4cm/1½ inches thick and lay
on a lightly greased baking sheet.

Mark the top into 4 sections and bake for 20 minutes until just
coloured and sounding hollow when tapped. Cool on a wire rack.
You could also add 1 tablespoon chopped parsley to the dough to
make a savoury accompaniment to stews and soups.

*This popular traditional bread, called a ran soide in Irish, is made using
buttermilk, which gives it a light texture and distinctive flavour. If you can't
find buttermilk, use plain yogurt instead. The raising agents are bicarbonate of
soda (baking soda) and cream of tartar, which react with the acids in the
buttermilk. The action is very quick, so it's essential to bake the bread
immediately. The secret of really good soda bread is to work quickly, handle
the dough gently, and bake in a hot oven.*

Boxty bread

225g/½ pound raw potatoes
225g/½ pound boiled potatoes
225g/½ pound plain (all-purpose) flour
½ teaspoon salt
Pinch of pepper
50g/½ stick butter

Preheat the oven to 180°C/350°F/gas mark 4.

Peel and grate the raw potatoes coarsely. Mash the boiled potatoes and blend in the grated potatoes, flour, salt and pepper. Stir in the melted butter and mix to a dough.

Turn the dough out onto a floured surface, but don't knead it. Divide the dough in half and press out each piece into a flat round. Place on greased baking trays and mark each piece into quarters; don't cut all the way through.

Bake for 30-40 minutes until cooked. Alternatively, cook the rounds on a hot greased griddle or heavy frying pan until cooked through. Break into quarters while hot and serve with plenty of good Irish butter.

There are lots of versions of boxty; bread, pancakes,
*dumplings and boxty (*bacstai *in Irish) in*
all its forms is a popular potato dish.
An old rhyme goes:

> *Boxty on the griddle*
> *Boxty in the pan*
> *If you don't eat your boxty*
> *You'll never get a man.*

Fadge

225g/½ pound freshly boiled potatoes
½ teaspoon salt
25g/¼ stick butter, melted
50g/2 ounces plain (all-purpose) flour

Mash the potatoes until smooth and free from lumps. Add the salt and melted butter, and then add the flour to form a dough.

Turn out onto a floured surface and roll or pat out the dough to 5mm/¼-inch thickness. Cut into rounds with a 7cm/2¾-inch cutter and cook on an ungreased hot griddle or heavy frying pan until browned on both sides.

Serve hot with plenty of butter. Fadge is also delicious with bacon and sausages for breakfast.

This potato bread from Ireland is known as 'fadge' in the northern counties. Be sure to use fresh, hot potatoes for this recipe to ensure that the finished bread is soft and light. Cold potatoes will produce bread with a heavy, leaden texture.

Buttermilk scones

450g/1 pound plain (all-purpose) flour
1 teaspoon baking powder
¼ teaspoon bicarbonate of soda (baking soda)
½ teaspoon salt
1 tablespoon sugar
150ml/⅝ cup buttermilk or natural yogurt
Milk or water

Preheat the oven to 200°C/400°F/gas mark 6.

Sift the dry ingredients into a mixing bowl and stir in
the buttermilk or yogurt and sufficient milk or water
to give a soft, smooth dough. Knead lightly and roll
out to about 1cm/½-inch thickness.

Cut into 5cm/2-inch rounds and place on a greased
baking tray. Brush with milk if you like a shiny finish.

Bake for 10-15 minutes, or until risen and lightly browned.
Cool on a wire rack.

Serve with butter, jam, preserves or honey.

Using buttermilk produces deliciously light scones with a spongy texture.
These are best eaten fresh on the day they're made.

Irish Johnny cakes

150g/5½ ounces medium oatmeal
50g/2 ounces plain (all-purpose) flour
1½ teaspoons baking powder
75g/¾ stick butter or margarine
1 tablespoon milk
75ml/generous ¼ cup clear honey
1 egg, beaten
50g/2 ounces raisins or sultanas (white raisins)

Preheat the oven to 200°C/400°F/gas mark 6. Grease a baking
tray or line it with non-stick baking paper.

In a mixing bowl, stir together the oatmeal, flour and baking
powder. Using your fingers, rub the butter into the flour mixture
until the mixture looks like fine breadcrumbs.

Heat the milk and honey in a small pan over a low heat until the
honey has melted. Pour this into the bowl and stir well. Stir the
egg into the mixture with the raisins or sultanas (white raisins),
stirring well.

Put spoonfuls of the mixture onto the baking tray, keeping them
well apart; they spread during cooking. Bake for 20 minutes, then
remove from the oven. Place the cakes on a
wire rack to cool.

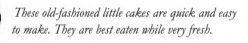

*These old-fashioned little cakes are quick and easy
to make. They are best eaten while very fresh.*

Irish porter cake

225g/2¼ sticks butter
225g/8 ounces molasses sugar (soft dark brown sugar)
3 eggs
350g/12 ounces plain (all-purpose) flour
1 teaspoon baking powder
2 teaspoons mixed spice
450g/1 pound mixed raisins, sultanas (white raisins) and currants
50g/2 ounces walnuts, chopped
150ml/⅝ cup Irish porter or stout (or other dark beer)

Preheat the oven to 160°C/325°F/gas mark 3. Grease and line a
deep 20cm/8-inch round cake tin (pan).

Cream the butter and sugar until light and fluffy. Beat in the eggs,
one at a time, and then sift in the flour, baking powder and spice.
Add the dried fruits and walnuts, followed by the porter.

Put into the cake tin and bake for 1 hour, then reduce the heat to
150°C/300°F/gas mark 2 and cook for another 1-2 hours, or
until cooked through.

Remove from the oven and leave to cool in the tin for about half
an hour before turning out.

Serve sliced with butter and/or cheese if desired.

*Irish porter and molasses sugar (soft dark brown sugar) impart a deep, dusky
richness to this moist, fruity cake, which tastes even better if left to mature for
a week before eating. Wrap the cake well and store in an airtight container.*

Irish cream liqueur and butter pudding

200g/2 sticks butter
10 thick slices of bread
115g/4 ounces mixed dried fruits (sultanas (white raisins), raisins,
  apricots, etc.)
50g/2 ounces roasted almonds, chopped
25g/1 ounce light muscovado (soft light brown) sugar
5 eggs
25g/1 ounce caster (superfine) sugar
200ml/⅞ cup milk
400ml/1¾ cups single (light) cream
6 tablespoons Irish cream liqueur
1 tablespoon demerara (light brown cane) sugar

Preheat the oven to 180°C/350°F/gas mark 4. Generously butter a large baking dish.

Spread the butter over the bread slices and cut into fingers or triangles. Place a layer of bread in the baking dish. Sprinkle with some of the fruits, almonds and light muscovado sugar. Repeat the layers until all the bread is used up.

Whisk the eggs and caster sugar in a bowl. Heat the milk and cream in a pan to boiling point and immediately remove from the heat. Slowly stir in the liqueur. Gradually pour the milk mixture into the eggs, stirring constantly. Pour over the bread in the baking dish and sprinkle with the demerara sugar.

Place the dish in a roasting tin (pan) and pour in hot water to 2.5cm/ 1 inch up the sides of the dish. Bake for 30-40 minutes, or until risen and golden. Serve hot, warm or cold with cream or custard.

Irish cream liqueur is delicious as a drink poured over ice or as in ingredient of cocktails. It also adds a glorious creamy richness in cooking.

Irish cream ice cream with Irish coffee sauce

500ml / 2⅓ cups double (heavy) cream
75g / 3 ounces icing (confectioner's) sugar
Pinch of salt
½ teaspoon vanilla essence
3 tablespoons Irish cream liqueur

For the Irish coffee sauce
225g / 8 ounces sugar
250ml / 1⅛ cups strong black coffee
2 tablespoons Irish whiskey

Put all the ingredients into a bowl and whisk until thick. Pour into a container, cover and freeze for 1 hour.

Tip the slushy mixture into a bowl and whisk to break down any ice crystals. Return to the freezer and repeat the process once more, then freeze until firm.

Place in the refrigerator 20 minutes to soften slightly before serving.

Irish coffee sauce: heat the sugar in a heavy-based pan with 2 teaspoons of water over a low heat until the sugar has dissolved. Increase the heat, bring to boiling point and boil without stirring until the syrup is pale gold.

Stir in the coffee and remove from the heat. Allow to cool and stir in the whiskey. Serve the ice cream drizzled with the sauce.

A delectably rich, creamy ice cream served trickled with a delicious sauce.

MOTHERING SUNDAY
(Mother's Day)

In the UK, the fourth Sunday of Lent is known as Mothering Sunday – nowadays the British equivalent, more or less, of the US Mother's Day. Originally it was one of the few days that servant girls were allowed home to visit their families. Centuries ago, it was considered important for people to return to their home or 'mother' church once a year. So each year in the middle of Lent, everyone would visit their 'mother' church, an event which eventually became an occasion for children working away from home to visit their families. It was usual in those days for children to leave home when still quite young and start work as servants or apprentices.

The origins of Mothering Sunday are much older than many people imagine. It was descended from the ancient Roman festival of Hilaria, or 'Mother of the Gods', on the Ides of March, when people made offerings in the temple. After the establishment of Christianity, the same festival was taken over by the Roman Catholic Church, and became Mothering Sunday, when the faithful were expected to make offerings to the 'mother Church'.

Traditionally, girls made a special cake for their mothers, and they usually took a fruited simnel cake home with them. Simnel cake became so associated with Mothering Sunday that the day itself became known as 'Simnel Sunday' in many areas. Nowadays simnel cake is baked only for Easter.

The day was a welcome break from the Lenten fast, and in some regions the day was also known as Refreshment Sunday. A special service was held at the 'mother church' for families, who then went home to enjoy a celebratory meal together. Usually this was roast veal or pork (or bacon for poorer families). A rich egg custard followed (eggs were forbidden during the rest of Lent) and sometimes a fig pudding. Dried figs were very popular and were displayed in shop windows at this time of year, ready to be put into little bags to give to children or make into puddings and pies.

In Lancashire, it was customary to drink 'bragger' or braggot: a heady mixture of spiced ale and honey, reputed to have been drunk by King Arthur and his knights at Camelot.

Mothering Sunday bears little connection to the American Mother's Day, although it has now become more widely known as 'Mother's Day' throughout Britain. Mother's Day in America began in 1872, when Julia Ward Howe organized a day for mothers dedicated to peace. Later, in 1907, Philadelphia schoolteacher Anna Jarvis (1864-1948) began a movement to set up a national Mother's Day in honour of her mother, Ann Maria Reeves Jarvis. She sought the help of hundreds of legislators and prominent businessmen to create a special day to honour mothers. The first Mother's Day observance was a church service in honour of Anna's mother, when Anna distributed white carnations, her mother's favourite flowers. Anna's efforts came to fruition in 1914, when President Woodrow Wilson proclaimed the second Sunday in May as a national holiday to honour mothers.

Today mothers are presented with presents, flowers and cards – and it's still a nice idea to make a special cake on Mother's Day.

Veal with cream sauce

675g/1½ pounds shoulder of veal, cubed
2 onions, chopped finely
2 carrots, chopped (optional)
Squeeze of lemon juice
1 bouquet garni
Salt and pepper
25g/¼ stick butter
25g/1 ounce flour
1 egg yolk
2-3 tablespoons single (light) cream

Put the veal, onions, carrots, lemon juice and the bouquet garni
into a large pan and season to taste. Add just enough water to
cover the ingredients and bring to the boil. Cover the pan and
simmer gently for about 1 hour, or until the meat is tender.

Strain off the cooking liquid, reserving 600ml/2½ cups. Keep the
meat and vegetables warm while you make the sauce.

Melt the butter in a pan and stir in the flour. Cook for 1 minute,
then remove from the heat and gradually stir in the reserved
liquid. Return to the heat and slowly bring to the boil, stirring
until the sauce thickens. Adjust the seasoning if necessary, and
then remove from the heat.

Allow to cool slightly, then stir in the egg yolk and cream. Stir in
the meat and vegetables and reheat for a few minutes, but do not
allow to boil or the mixture will curdle. Serve immediately.

Veal in a creamy sauce makes a perfect Mothering Sunday meal. Milk-fed
veal has a delicate flavour, a very tender, juicy texture, and doesn't shrink
much during cooking. Take care not to overcook it, however, or the meat will
dry out and become tough.

Veal with wine sauce

(Bradford Family Recipe)

6 x 115g/4-ounce veal fillets
Salt and pepper
1 tablespoon flour
110g/1 stick butter
6 shallots, finely chopped
8 tablespoons dry white wine
8 tablespoons port
8 tablespoons stock

Season the veal with salt and pepper and toss in the flour to coat
lightly. Heat half the butter in a shallow pan and sear the fillets on
both sides until browned. Reduce the heat and cook slowly for
10-15 minutes, or until cooked through. Remove from the pan
and keep warm.

Add the shallots to the pan and cook gently until softened. Stir in
the white wine and port and cook steadily until reduced by half.

Add the stock and heat until hot but not boiling. Remove from the
heat and stir in the remaining butter gradually. Place the veal on
warmed serving plates and spoon over the sauce. Serve immediately.

Veal is so underappreciated in Britain – something I can never understand.
It is a delightful meat to cook with because it absorbs the flavours of what
it is combined with more readily than beef. Hence this wonderfully rich
mixture: a special dish of my mother's. RB

Roast pork with apples and pears

1.5kg/3 pound 5 ounce joint of pork
1 tablespoon oil
Salt and pepper
3 eating (dessert) apples
3 firm pears
150ml/⅝ cup apple juice
150ml/⅝ cup stock or water
3 tablespoons flour
2 tablespoons cider (applejack) or white wine
2 tablespoons quince or redcurrant jelly

Preheat the oven to 190°C/375°F/gas mark 5.

Brush the pork rind with the oil and sprinkle with salt. Place the joint on a rack in a roasting tin (pan) and cook in the oven for 30 minutes, then reduce the heat to 180°C/350°F/gas mark 4 and cook for another hour.

Core the apples and pears and cut into quarters. Remove the roasting tin from the oven, pour off the fat (reserve for later) and place the fruit in the tin, underneath the rack. Pour in the apple juice and return to the oven for 30 minutes, or until the fruit and the meat are tender. Place the joint on a warmed serving dish with the fruit and keep it warm while you make the gravy.

Pour the liquid from the tin into a measuring jug and make up to 300ml/1¼ cups with the stock. Place 2 tablespoons of the reserved fat into a pan, stir in the flour, then the cider and cook for 1 minute. Gradually add the stock, bring to the boil and cook for 2 minutes. Stir in the jelly and season with salt and pepper to taste.

Tender pork is perfectly complemented with delicious apples and pears and gravy with a hint of fruity sweetness from the quince or redcurrant jelly.

Rhubarb and apple sauce

4 sticks rhubarb, chopped
1 eating (dessert) apple, peeled cored and chopped
Sugar to taste
25g/¼ stick butter

Put the rhubarb and apple in a pan with the sugar and butter.
Cover and cook over a low heat until the fruit is soft and tender.

Taste and add more sugar if needed. Beat to a smooth pulp
and serve.

This lovely pink sauce is delicious with rich, fatty meats and poultry such as
pork and duck. Although, strictly speaking, rhubarb is a vegetable, it's
widely regarded in the UK as one of the first fruits of spring.

Sugar baked figs

½ teaspoon vanilla extract
50ml/¼ cup white wine
Enough figs to fit closely into a baking dish
Caster (superfine) sugar

Preheat the oven to 220°C/425°F/gas mark 7.

Mix the vanilla with the wine. Dip the figs in the wine and vanilla, then roll each one in sugar until well coated. Put the figs into the baking dish and cook for about 15-20 minutes, or until the sugar and juices have formed a rich brown syrup at the bottom of the dish.

Remove from the oven and leave to cool. Chill well befo re serving with whipped cream or ice cream.

Use fresh unpeeled soft, ripe figs for this recipe. The best are Smyrna-type figs, which have a coating of crystallized natural sugars.

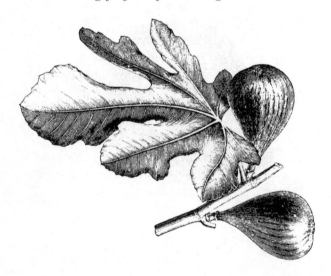

Rosemary and lemon sandwich cake

175g/1¾ stick butter
175g/6 ounces caster (superfine) sugar
3 eggs, separated
150g/5½ ounces self-raising (self-rising) flour
25g/1 ounce cornflour (cornstarch)
1 tablespoon chopped fresh rosemary, plus a few sprigs
  to decorate
Finely grated zest of 1 small lemon
150ml/⅝ cup whipping cream
Icing (confectioner's) sugar for dusting

Preheat the oven to 170°C/325°F/gas mark 3. Grease a 20cm/
8-inch round cake tin (pan) and sprinkle lightly with a little flour.

Cream the butter with 115g/4 ounces sugar until light and creamy.
Whisk in the egg yolks. Sift together the flour and cornflour and
fold into the mixture.

Whisk the egg whites until they form soft peaks and whisk in the
remaining sugar. Gently fold half this meringue into the cake
mixture until incorporated, then fold in the other half with the
rosemary and lemon zest. Spoon into the prepared tin and bake
for 1-1½ hours, testing with a skewer, which should come out
clean. Cool in the tin for 15 minutes, then turn out onto a wire
rack to become cold.

Whip the cream until thick but not stiff. Split the cake in half
and sandwich with the cream. Dust the top of the cake with icing
sugar and decorate with sprigs of rosemary.

Any mum will love the refreshing aromatic flavour of this lovely light cake
which is sandwiched with fresh whipped cream.

Unbelievably rich chocolate cake

300g/10 ounces plain (dark) chocolate (at least 70% cocoa solids)
250g/2½ sticks unsalted butter
2 tablespoons strong black coffee
200g/7 ounces caster (superfine) sugar
6 large eggs, separated
100g/3½ ounces plain (all-purpose) flour
Cocoa powder for dusting
225g/8 ounces raspberries

Preheat the oven to 200°C/400°F/gas mark 6. Grease a 23cm/
9-inch springform cake tin (pan).

Melt together the chocolate, butter and coffee in a heatproof bowl
over a pan of simmering (not boiling) water, or in a microwave
oven. Allow to cool.

Whisk the sugar with the egg yolks until pale and thick. Gently
fold in the chocolate mixture along with the flour.

Whisk the egg whites until stiff but not dry and fold into the
mixture, until thoroughly incorporated with no streaks remaining.
Pour into the prepared tin and bake for 20-25 minutes, or until
the edges are set, but the centre is still soft.

Leave to cool, then wrap in foil or cling film (plastic wrap) and
leave at room temperature for a day before cutting. Dust the
top with cocoa powder and place on a serving plate surrounded
by raspberries.

*A sumptuous, very chocolatey cake, perfectly complemented by the slight
tartness of the raspberries. You need to make this the day before you want to
eat it as it ought to stand for a day before cutting.*

Orange and spice dessert cake

1 teaspoon ground cinnamon
1 teaspoon ground mixed spice
1 teaspoon crushed cardamom seeds
Grated zest and juice of 1 large orange
115g/4 ounces ground almonds
50g/2 ounces fresh white breadcrumbs
75g/3 ounces sugar
4 eggs, separated
Pinch of salt
1 teaspoon orange-flower water
Whipped cream and grated orange zest to finish

Preheat the oven to 190°C/375°F/gas mark 5. Butter an 18cm/7-inch loose-based cake tin (pan).

Mix the spices with the orange zest and juice, ground almonds, breadcrumbs and sugar. Beat the egg yolks and stir into the mixture. Whisk the egg whites and salt until stiff but not dry and gently fold into the mixture.

Pour into the prepared tin and bake for about 40 minutes until cooked through. Cool in the tin.

Turn out and sprinkle the top of the cake with orange-flower water. Spread the top of the cake with whipped cream and grated orange zest.

This light but luscious cake contains no fat. You can
omit the whipped-cream topping if you prefer.

Orange blossom cake

225g/2¼ sticks unsalted butter
400g/14 ounces caster (superfine) sugar
4 eggs
1 tablespoon orange-flower water
350g/12 ounces plain (all-purpose) flour
4 teaspoons baking powered
Pinch of salt
225ml/1 cup milk
Finely grated zest 1 orange

For the filling
600g/1 pound 5 ounces orange marmalade
150ml/⅝ cup double (heavy) cream, whipped
3 tablespoons golden icing (confectioner's) sugar to finish

Preheat the oven to 180°C/350°F/gas mark 4. Grease 3 x 23cm/ 9-inch round cake tins (pans) and line them with greaseproof (waxed) paper.

Cream the butter and sugar together until light and pale. Beat in the eggs gradually, beating well. Stir in the orange-flower water. Sift in the flour, baking powder and salt and gently stir until incorporated. Gradually stir in the milk, followed by the orange zest, mixing gently.

Divide the mixture evenly among the prepared tins and bake for about 20-30 minutes, or until cooked and springy to the touch. Cool in the tins for 15 minutes, then turn out carefully onto a wire rack to become cold.

Place one cake on a serving plate and spread with half the marmalade. Spread half the cream on top and place another cake layer on top. Repeat with the remaining marmalade and cream and top with the third cake. Sift the icing sugar over the top.

A perfect cake for a spring day, scented with sweet, flowery orange-flower water.

Chocolate banana loaf cake

3 medium-sized ripe bananas
175g/6 ounces light muscovado (soft light brown) sugar
175g/6 ounces self-raising (self-rising) flour
2 eggs, beaten
3 tablespoons sunflower oil
55ml/¼ cup milk
115g/4 ounces chocolate, chopped
75g/3 ounces walnuts, chopped

Preheat the oven to 180°C/350°F/gas mark 4. Grease a 20 x 10cm/8 x 4 inch loaf tin (pan).

In a mixing bowl, mash the bananas with the sugar until smooth. Stir in the flour, eggs, oil and milk, mixing well until everything is thoroughly combined. Gently stir in the chocolate and walnuts.

Pour into the prepared tin and cook for 50-60 minutes, or until cooked through. Test by inserting a skewer into the centre of the cake; if it comes out clean with no mixture clinging to it, it is cooked. Remove from the oven and cool in the tin for 5 minutes. Turn out onto a wire rack and leave until cold.

A wonderfully moist loaf packed with chocolate, bananas and nuts. Its makes a terrific quick dessert sliced and topped with a scoop of vanilla or chocolate ice cream.

Hummingbird cake

250g/9 ounces self-raising (self-rising) flour
200g/7 ounces caster sugar
½ teaspoon salt
1 teaspoon ground cinnamon
2 eggs
225ml/1 cup sunflower oil
1 teaspoon vanilla extract
250g/9 ounces ripe bananas (peeled weight)
115g/4 ounces walnuts, chopped
1 x 175g/6-ounce can crushed pineapple

<u>For the filling and topping</u>
175g/1¾ sticks unsalted butter
1 teaspoon vanilla extract
350g/12 ounces golden icing (confectioner's) sugar

Preheat the oven to 180°C/350°F/gas mark 4. Grease 2 x 20cm/ 8-inch round cake tins (pans); line with greaseproof (waxed) paper.

Mix the dry ingredients in a mixing bowl. Beat the eggs with the oil and vanilla extract. Mash the bananas and stir into the mixture with the walnuts and the pineapple, including the juice.

Mix well to combine, then pour into the prepared tins. Bake for 30-35 minutes until light golden brown. Cool in the tins for a few minutes, then turn out onto a wire rack to become cold.

For the filling and topping, cream together the butter and vanilla until soft. Sift in the golden icing sugar gradually and beat well. Use half to sandwich the cakes together, then spread the rest on top. Decorate with fresh spring flowers

This lusciously moist cake originated in the USA. The name came about because it contains fruits which hummingbirds love.

No need to cook chocolate cake

300g/10½ ounces plain (dark) chocolate (at least 70% cocoa solids),
* broken into pieces*
115g/1 stick unsalted butter
50g/2 ounces light muscovado (soft light brown) sugar
115g/4 ounces shortbread biscuits (cookies), broken into small pieces
115g/4 ounces glacé (candied) cherries, halved
75g/3 ounces whole roasted hazelnuts
75g/3 ounces almonds, roughly chopped

Line an 18cm/7-inch round cake tin (pan) with non-stick
baking paper.

Melt the chocolate, butter and sugar in a bowl over a pan of
simmering (not boiling) water or in a microwave oven. Leave to
cool but not starting to set.

Stir in the remaining ingredients and turn into the prepared tin,
pressing down gently. Leave to set at room temperature until firm.

Remove the cake from the tin and peel away the paper. Cut into
thin wedges to serve.

This fabulously munchy, crunchy cake is so easy and quick to make, a child
could make it – with adult supervision.

White chocolate rochers

225g/8 ounces slivered almonds
115g/4 ounces golden icing (confectioner's) sugar
2 tablespoons liqueur, e.g. Cointreau
225g/8 ounces white chocolate

Preheat the oven to as 180°C/350°F/gas mark 4. Line a tray with non-stick baking paper.

In a bowl, mix together the almonds, icing sugar and liqueur, stirring well to combine.

Spread the mixture on a baking tray and bake for 20 minutes, stirring every 5 minutes until the mixture has browned and crystallized. Leave to cool, and then break into 20-24 pieces.

Melt the chocolate in a bowl over a pan of hot (not boiling) water or in a microwave oven. Dip each piece into the chocolate. Place on the lined tray and leave until set, then place in paper or foil sweet (candy) cases.

These nutty, crunchy little chocolate rocks would make a delightful present for Mother's Day. They're also delicious with coffee at the end of a meal.

EASTER

Throughout Britain, many ancient Easter customs still take place, such as egg-rolling and the time-honoured custom of the Biddenden Dole held every Easter Monday (the Monday following Easter Sunday is a UK holiday) at Biddenden in Kent. Here, Biddenden cakes are distributed as part of an ancient charity. Each cake bears a picture of two females who are joined on one side. These are said to be Siamese twins Eliza and Mary Chulkhurst, born in 1100, who bequeathed money for the 'dole' of beer, bread, cheese and cakes. When one of the sisters died at the age of 34, the other refused to be separated from her and died six hours later.

They left 20 acres of ground called the 'Bread and Cheese Lands' to provide money for the Dole Morris dancers ('Morris', it is said, comes from Moorish dancers of Spain) to perform their dances and spring rituals for the fertility of the land, which were regarded as an ancient tradition, even in the Elizabethan era. Oliver Cromwell banned the 'madde men' with their 'Devils dance' following the Civil War, but they made a welcome reappearance after the Restoration.

The Easter Monday hare-pie scramble in Hallaton in Leicestershire dates back to the eighteenth century and begins with the parading of a giant 'hare' pie, actually made of beef these days. Hallaton's vicar blesses the pie before it is cut and given to the crowd. After that, the bottle-kicking contest (which curiously involves neither bottles nor kicking) between Hallaton and nearby Medbourne can start. The two village teams face each other at Hare Pie Bank and fight over three small beer barrels. The object of the no-holds-barred contest is to get the barrels to the village boundary. Both teams share the beer contained within the final cask.

The belief that the sun bowed or danced in honour of Christ's Resurrection on Easter Sunday was once widespread. It was thought that anyone who went up to the top of a high hill early in the morning to watch the sunrise would see the sun bow two or three times. This custom was well established in Wales, where on Easter Monday crowds formed a procession to the top of the nearest mountain to watch the sun rise.

After the long Lenten fast, Easter foods – meat, eggs, cream, cheese and butter ... all the foods denied in Lent – appeared in abundance in many kinds of delicious dishes. In medieval England roast lamb and apple fritters were traditional fare, along with duck, spinach tarts and clotted cream. Easter ledger pudding, a savoury dish made with spring herbs, was also eaten with roast veal.

Richly fruited and lightly spiced simnel cake is traditionally enjoyed at Easter and is different to any other celebratory fruit cake because of a middle and top layer of almond paste. In medieval England, simnel was a light bread made from fine flour and either baked twice or first boiled and then baked. By the mid-sixteenth century, spices, dried fruit and sometimes saffron were added to enrich the bread dough. Simnels, like other cakes, were made by bakers, who flourished in Britain's towns and villages.

In the Lancashire town of Bury, the cakes were called 'simblins'. Early versions were large teacakes, rather like fruited bread and completely different to the type we know today. Other regions produced their own versions of simnel cakes, usually of lightly spiced, fruited yeast dough. In Shropshire and Herefordshire, the rich dough was first boiled in a cloth, then enclosed in a crust and baked, while simnel cakes in Worcestershire were enriched with saffron as well as dried fruits.

Eggs have long been associated with Easter, although they have an even longer association with spring and fertility in pagan traditions, and were 'borrowed' by the early Christian Church, where they were thought to symbolize life. In Mesopotamia, children dyed eggs yellow and green, and also red in memory of the blood of Christ. Scarlet-coloured eggs were given as gifts in Greece and Syria.

The Crusaders came across these customs on their travels and brought them back to England. By the thirteenth century, it had become customary to exchange gifts of coloured hard-boiled eggs on Easter Sunday. The household accounts of Edward I for 1290 include an entry of 18 pence spent on 'four hundred and a half of eggs' which were to be 'covered with leaf-gold or stained by boiling', then distributed to members of the royal household. Gold leaf was a costly decoration; it was more common to use plants, mosses or other natural substances to impart colour. The eggs were dyed by boiling with a natural dye such as onion skins, which produced a golden-brown egg; beetroot (beet) juice for red; and logwood chips for a rich, purplish blue.

Sometimes hard-boiled eggs were painted or gilded to make an eye-catching colourful display, which would be kept throughout Easter week. There are several coloured eggs in the Wordsworth Museum at Grasmere which were originally decorated for the poet's children. Families took hard-boiled eggs to their local church to be blessed at Easter, and afterwards these 'holy' eggs were taken home and placed in the centre of the table, surrounded by large platters of meat. The best tableware was also used to honour the Easter eggs, and visitors were invited to eat one – a great treat after the long Lenten fast, when eggs were forbidden. The end of the Lenten fast was celebrated with a great Easter Sunday feast, which included boiled eggs served with green herb sauce. Eggs were also made into silky custards; in Kent, a particular delicacy was Kentish pudding pie – a rich custard tart.

'Pace egging' was a popular practice of begging for eggs and other foods from houses and farms, usually by children in costume or small groups of men. The latter would perform a 'pace-egg play', a semi-ritual enactment of death and rebirth, or would dress as some popular characters from Christian or secular history – for instance, St George or Admiral Nelson. The word 'pace' is derived from *Pesach*, the Hebrew word for 'Passover' and was the common name for Easter.

In Scotland, pace eggs were greatly prized by young boys who played a game with them that was very similar to the British custom of 'conkers' – but instead of using horse chestnuts, the object here was to smash one's rival's egg. Until fairly recently in Scotland, Easter Sunday was called Pass or Pasch Sunday.

A typical pace-egging rhyme was:

> *Now we're jolly pace-eggers all in one round,*
> *We've come a pace–egging, we hope you'll prove kind.*
> *We hope you'll prove kind with some eggs and some beer,*
> *For we'll come no more near you 'til it is next year.*

Egg-rolling was a favourite sport at Easter, popular in both Britain and America. Hard-boiled eggs were rolled down a hill or slope and the winner was the egg that rolled the furthest, or survived the most rolls without cracking. In the USA, it has been the custom since 1877 for the president to take part in egg-rolling on the White House lawns; hard-boiled eggs are rolled downhill and the last uncracked egg remaining wins the prize.

By the seventeenth and eighteenth centuries, coloured hard-boiled eggs were replaced by egg-shaped toys for children, and by the nineteenth century the toys were gradually ousted by Victorian cardboard and satin eggs filled with chocolates and other sweets. In England, J. S. Fry (now part of the Cadbury empire) created the first chocolate Easter eggs in 1873, made of dark chocolate and filled with sweets. Cadbury's produced the first Dairy Milk chocolate egg in 1905. Chocolate Easter eggs were and remain a phenomenal success; over 80 million Easter eggs are now sold in the UK every year!

Scottish baked eggs

75g/3 ounces fresh white breadcrumbs
4 eggs
25g/¼ stick butter
Salt and pepper
115g/4 ounces mature Cheddar cheese, grated
300ml/1¼ cups double (heavy) cream

Preheat the oven to 190°C/375°F/gas mark 5.

Butter a baking dish. Scatter half the breadcrumbs over the base of the dish. Break the eggs into the dish and scatter with more breadcrumbs. Dot with the butter and season to taste.

Sprinkle with the cheese and the rest of the breadcrumbs. Pour over the cream and bake for 15–20 minutes, or until bubbling.

This is an old farmhouse recipe from Scotland for a luxurious savoury dish of eggs, cheese and breadcrumbs baked in cream.

Watercress soup

25g/¼ stick butter
1 tablespoon oil
1 onion, finely chopped
750g/1 pound 10 ounces potatoes, peeled and diced
1 litre/4½ cups vegetable stock or water
1 bunch or bag of watercress
Salt and pepper
Fresh cream (optional)

Heat the butter and oil in a large pan and add the onion and potato. Cover and cook for 10 minutes, or until softened, stirring occasionally.

Add the stock or water, cover and bring to the boil. Simmer for 15-20 minutes, or until the vegetables are cooked. Pour into a blender or food processor and add the watercress. Process until blended. Season to taste with salt and pepper.

Reheat gently and pour into bowls. Add a swirl of cream to each bowl just before serving.

Watercress, once a mere garnish, is now recognized as a delicious and health-giving vegetable. Its pungent flavour enhances soups, sauces and flavoured butters.

Spring herb pudding

450g/1 pound mixed fresh young greens or spring herbs of your choice,
 finely chopped
1 onion, finely chopped
50g/2 ounces pearl barley
175g/6 ounces oatmeal
½ teaspoon salt
2 or 3 eggs, beaten
4 tablespoons butter
Salt and pepper
Oil for frying

Butter a large pudding basin or heatproof mixing bowl. Mix
together the leaves, onion, barley, oatmeal and salt. Put into the
pudding basin and cover with a tight-fitting lid or greaseproof
(waxed) paper and foil tied securely. Boil or steam for 2 hours.

Turn out into a large mixing bowl and beat in the eggs, butter, salt
and pepper. Shape into a flat cake.

Heat the oil in a frying pan until hot, then fry the cake until browned
on both sides, turning halfway through cooking. Serve immediately
with roast lamb, bacon and eggs, etc.

Country people in days gone by ate this pudding as a spring tonic after their
monotonous winter diet. Young spring leaves are a natural blood purifier and
also contain iron as well as vitamins A and C. Use any edible seasonal
freshly picked young leaves such as nettles, hawthorn, wild garlic, watercress,
lettuce, dandelion, strawberry, raspberry, etc. Pick young, tender leaves from
an unpolluted spot, well away from roadside exhaust fumes and roaming
dogs. Wash the leaves well before using.

Asparagus flan

225g/8 ounces shortcrust (medium-flake) pastry
450ml/2 cups whipping cream
3 eggs
Salt and pepper
1 bundle of cooked asparagus
3 tablespoons freshly grated Parmesan cheese

Preheat the oven to 200°C/400°F/gas mark 6.

Grease a deep 22cm/8½-inch flan or pie dish or tin. Roll out the pastry and line the dish. Bake blind for 15 minutes. Remove the pastry case from the oven and leave to cool.

Reduce the oven temperature to 180°C/350°F/gas mark 4. Whisk the cream and eggs together and season to taste with salt and pepper. Place the cooked, cooled asparagus in the pastry case and sprinkle with the cheese. Pour over the egg mixture. Cook for 20-30 minutes, or until the custard is just set. Serve warm with a green salad.

The appearance of the new season's asparagus is eagerly anticipated in the cook's calendar. The plump, green spears add a touch of luxury to meals. A member of the lily family, asparagus got its name from the Greek word meaning 'stalk' or 'shoot'.

Roast lamb with red wine gravy

1 leg of lamb, approximately 2kg/4½ pounds
Salt and pepper

For the gravy
2 tablespoons pan juices
1 tablespoon plain (all-purpose) flour
150ml/⅝ cup red wine
300ml/1¼ cups stock or water
1 tablespoon redcurrant jelly (use quince if unavailable)
Grated zest and juice of 1 small orange

Preheat the oven to 180°C/350°F/gas mark 4.

Place the lamb in a roasting tin (pan) and season with salt and pepper. Roast for 20 minutes per 450g/pound, plus 20 minutes. Keep warm while you make the gravy.

Pour the pan juices into a saucepan and stir in the flour. Cook over a low heat for 2 minutes until thickened. Gradually add the wine and stock or water, stirring all the time and bring to the boil. Simmer for 10 minutes, and then add the redcurrant jelly, orange zest and juice. Simmer for another 2 minutes and adjust the seasoning to taste before serving with the lamb.

Serve with boiled new potatoes, garden peas and carrots.

Red wine and orange juice and zest add a particularly delicious flavour to the lamb. Orange juice was often used to baste lamb and mutton in the eighteenth century.

Duck with oranges

1 oven-ready duck, approx 1.5kg/3 pounds 5 ounces in weight
1 tablespoon flour
Salt and pepper
25g/¼ stick butter
1 orange, peeled and thinly sliced
½ lemon, peeled and thinly sliced
25g/1 ounce flour
400ml/1¾ cups stock
Rind and juice of 2 oranges
Rind and juice of ½ lemon
1 tablespoon sherry

Preheat the oven to 200°C/400°F/gas mark 6. Rub the bird with flour, salt and pepper. Put the orange and lemon slices inside the duck and place in a roasting tin (pan). Cook for 20 minutes, then remove from the oven and prick the skin (not the flesh) with a sharp knife; this allows the fat to run out and the skin to crisp.

Return to the oven and reduce the temperature to 170°C/350°F/gas mark 3 and cook for another 20 minutes. Prick the skin again and return to the oven for a further 20 minutes, by which time the duck should be cooked. Keep hot.

Remove the pith from the orange and lemon rinds and cut the rind into thin strips. Place in a pan with a cupful of water and boil for 15 minutes. Crush the peel with a fork; stir in the sherry.

Pour off the fat from the roasting tin and stir in the flour. Add the peel, sherry, stock, orange and lemon juices to the tin and cook over a low heat for 2-3 minutes. Taste and adjust the seasoning. Serve the sauce with the duck.

This bittersweet sauce is the perfect accompaniment to rich, succulent duck meat. Serve with new potatoes and green vegetables for an appetizing Easter meal.

Gooseberry sauce

225g/8 ounces green gooseberries
2 tablespoons water or dry white wine
Few sprigs fresh mint
Pinch of salt
50g/2 ounces caster (superfine) sugar
25g/¼ stick butter

Put the gooseberries into a pan (there's no need to top and tail them) with the water or wine and mint. Bring to the boil, cover the pan and simmer gently until tender.

Push the mixture through a sieve and return the purée to the pan. Add the salt, sugar and butter and simmer for 5 minutes, stirring.

Serve with roast pork and duck, as well as mackerel. The tartness cuts through the richness of the meat and fish.

When raw, the small hard green berries are sharp and sour-tasting, but their acidity is transformed by cooking them with sugar. This beautiful bright-green sauce is delicious with roast pork and duck, as well as mackerel. The tartness cuts through the richness of the meat and fish.

Gooseberries have been cultivated in England since the thirteenth century and were very popular in Tudor times. Their name may come from the fact that the Tudors and Elizabethans used the berries in stuffings for roast goose. Alternatively, the name may come from the French word groseille, *meaning 'currant'. In Scotland, where the country's history has strong French links, gooseberries are often called 'grossets'.*

Beer battered baked apples

50g/2 ounces plain (all-purpose) flour
Pinch of salt
1 tablespoon sugar plus extra for sprinkling
150ml/⅝ cup beer
1 tablespoon melted butter
1 egg, plus 2 egg whites
2-3 eating (dessert) apples
Oil for deep frying

Mix the flour, salt and sugar in a mixing bowl and stir in the beer.
Gently stir in the butter and whole egg. Leave the mixture to
stand for 1 hour.

Whisk the egg whites until stiff and fold into the mixture. Peel
and roughly chop the apples and gently stir them into the batter.

Heat the oil in a deep-fat fryer or deep pan, drop spoonfuls of
the mixture into the fat and cook until crisp and golden: about
3-5 minutes. Drain on kitchen paper (paper towels) and sprinkle
with sugar. Serve hot.

*The batter is left to stand for an hour so that any elasticity disappears. The
egg whites must be added just before cooking to ensure that the batter is light
and airy. Use a golden, medium-strength beer for best results.*

Kentish pudding pie

250g/9 ounces shortcrust (medium-flake) pastry
300ml/1¼ cups milk
Strip of lemon peel
40g/1½ ounces ground rice
Pinch of salt
50g/½ stick butter
50g/2 ounces sugar
2 eggs
25g/1 ounce currants

Preheat the oven to 200°C/400°F/gas mark 6.

Roll out the pastry about 1.5cm/⅝-inch thick and line a baking dish. Bake blind (prick the base and place a piece of greaseproof [waxed] paper with some baking beans on the pastry). Bake for 10-15 minutes, then allow to cool.

Reduce the oven temperature to 180°C/350°F/gas mark 4.

Heat most of the milk slowly with the lemon peel and bring to the boil. Mix the ground rice with the remaining cold milk and salt until smooth. Stir into the hot milk and bring to the boil, stirring constantly. Simmer gently for 5 minutes, stirring to prevent the mixture sticking to the pan.

Remove from the heat and beat in the butter and sugar. Allow to cool slightly, then beat in the eggs, mixing thoroughly. Stir in the currants. Pour into the pastry case. Bake for about 40-45 minutes, or until the filling is firm and golden brown. Serve warm.

Some old recipes use puff pastry instead of shortcrust, but crisp shortcrust pastry works better with the smooth custard filling. In Kent, these pies were served at Easter with strong cherry ale.

Chocolate fudge nut flan

50g/½ stick unsalted butter
175g/6 ounces digestive biscuits (graham crackers), crushed

For the filling
250g/9 ounces light muscovado (soft light brown) sugar
150ml/⅝ cup water
50g/½ stick butter
50g/2 ounces hazelnuts, chopped
150ml/⅝ cup double (heavy) cream
50g/2 ounces plain (dark) chocolate

Grease a 20cm/8-inch flan tin or pie dish.

Melt the butter and mix with the biscuit crumbs. Press into the base and sides of the tin or dish and chill until needed.

Put the sugar and water into a pan and heat gently until the sugar has dissolved. Bring to the boil and simmer without stirring until the mixture is a straw-coloured caramel. Remove from the heat and stir in the butter, hazelnuts and all but 2 teaspoons of the cream.

Return to the heat and bring to the boil. Simmer for 10 minutes until thickened. Remove from the heat and allow to cool a little before pouring into the flan case. Leave to cool.

Melt the chocolate and stir in the remaining cream. Spread over the filling and chill for at least 2 hours before serving.

The crunchiness of the not-too-sweet crust balances the smooth, dense chocolate filling. Serve in small slices – this tart is very rich.

Spinach tart

225g/8 ounces shortcrust (medium-flake) pastry
1 kg/2¼ pounds fresh spinach, well-washed and drained
2 tablespoons white wine
4 large apples
3 tablespoons sugar
1 teaspoon orange-flower water
1 teaspoon ground mixed spice

Preheat the oven to 200°C/400°F/gas mark 6.

Roll out the pastry and line a 28cm/11-inch flan tin or pie dish.
Bake blind for 10 minutes, then remove any beans and reduce the
heat to 180°C/350°F/gas mark 4 and cook for another 10
minutes. Remove from the oven and leave to cool.

Put the spinach into a large pan with the wine over a low heat and
cook for a few minutes until wilted and very tender. Drain well and
put into a food processor or blender and blend to a purée. Add the
sugar, orange-flower water and spices and tip the mixture into a
pan. Bring to the boil and simmer gently until the mixture is thick.

Spoon into the pastry case and serve cold.

Many recipes for 'spinage' tart appeared in Elizabethan times.

Violet ice cream

200g/7 ounces caster (superfine) sugar
450ml/2 cups water
Juice of 1 lemon
75ml/generous ¼ cup crème de violette (violet liqueur)
150ml/⅝ cup double (heavy) cream
25g/1 ounce crystallized violets

Heat the sugar and water in a pan over a low heat until the sugar
has dissolved completely. Bring to the boil and boil rapidly for 3
minutes, then remove from the heat and leave to cool.

Stir in the lemon juice, pour into a freezer-proof container and
freeze until half-frozen and slushy.

Tip the mixture into a bowl and beat well. Stir in the liqueur.
Whisk the cream until thick and softly peaking and gently fold
into the mixture with most of the crystallized violets. Return to
the freezer and freeze until firm.

Transfer the mixture to the refrigerator to soften about 30
minutes before serving. Scatter with crystallized violets to serve.

Sweetly scented violets bloom in the spring and have been admired for their
delicate beauty and fragrance since antiquity. Crystallized violet petals also
make a pretty decoration for cakes and desserts. The fragile flowers are
immersed in sugar syrup, boiled and left to crystallize.

Rich chocolate mousse

(Bradford Family Recipe)

225g/8 ounces bitter (plain or baking) chocolate, at least 70% cocoa solids
8 eggs, separated
1 teaspoon brandy

Melt the chocolate in a heatproof bowl over a pan of simmering (not boiling) water, or in a microwave oven. Allow to cool.

Whisk the yolks until thickened and fold into the chocolate, stirring until well mixed. Whisk the egg whites until stiff but not dry and gently stir into the chocolate mixture.

Add the brandy and pour into a serving dish or individual dishes. Chill in the fridge for 24 hours before serving.

This is so easy to put together, and always proves to be hugely popular. Why bother adding cream, sugar or gelatine when simple and straightforward really is the best way with chocolate mousse? You can also adjust the recipe to make it richer by using one or two fewer eggs – or indeed go in the opposite direction if you want it to be lighter. RB

Chocolate Easter nest cake

110g/1 stick butter
275g/9½ ounces dark muscovado (soft dark brown) sugar
2 eggs, beaten
175g/6 ounces plain (all-purpose) flour
½ teaspoon baking powder
1 teaspoon bicarbonate of soda (baking soda)
200ml/1 cup dark beer or stout (or other dark beer)
50g/2 ounces cocoa powder

For the filling and topping
25g/1 ounce cocoa powder
3 tablespoons boiling water
175g/1¾ sticks butter
250-350g/9-12 ounces golden icing (confectioner's) sugar, sifted

4-6 chocolate Cadbury's Flake bars (use chocolate shavings if unavailable)
to decorate
115g/4 ounces chocolate mini eggs

Preheat the oven to 180°C/350°F/gas mark 4. Grease a 20cm/
8-inch round deep cake tin (pan) and line the base with greaseproof
(waxed) paper.

Cream the butter and sugar together until soft, then beat in the
eggs. Sift the flour, baking powder and soda into a bowl. Mix the
stout and cocoa powder together.

Fold the flour and cocoa mixtures alternately into the butter
mixture until well combined. Spoon into the prepared cake tin
and bake for about 1 hour, or until cooked through. Cool slightly
in the tin, then turn out and cool on a wire rack.

To make the filling and topping, mix the cocoa powder with the boiling water to make a paste. Cream the butter until soft and creamy, then beat in the icing sugar, beating really well (an electric mixer is ideal) until light. Stir in the cooled cocoa.

Split the cake in half and sandwich it with about a third of the icing mixture. Spread the remaining butter-cream over the top and sides of the cake, making a hollow 'nest' in the centre.

Crumble the chocolate flake bars and press lightly into the butter-cream. Fill the hollow with chocolate mini eggs.

It wouldn't be Easter without chocolate! This 'nest' is a soft, moist cake made with stout, which enhances the chocolate flavour.

Summer

MAY DAY

In the calendar of the ancient Celts, the first day of summer was celebrated with bonfires – the 'fire of Bel', or Beltane – to welcome the return of the sun, together with the wider variety of foods that appeared after the cold, dark days of winter. Ancient Britons erected wooden poles festooned with flowers in honour of the goddess of spring to herald the new season. By the Middle Ages, every town and village had its own brightly painted maypole, gaily decorated with flowers, ribbons and streamers. The maypole set up in Aldgate, London, beside St Andrew's Church was so large that it overshadowed the church and the church became known as St Andrew Undershaft.

Everyone got up early on May morning and went into the woods and countryside to collect branches and flowers to decorate their homes. Chaucer wrote that those who resided at the fifteenth-century court of Henry VI rose early and went out to gather flowers and greenery to decorate the rooms. The court dignitaries later gathered at Stebunheath (Stepney) for a grand dinner.

Henry VIII and Queen Catherine of Aragon celebrated May Day at Greenwich in 1515 with their court and nobles. The queen, accompanied by 25 of her ladies, went out at dawn to gather the dew for the purpose of preserving her complexion. A contemporary account describes how later in the day, Catherine and her retinue rode into a wood two miles from Greenwich to meet the king 'with his guard all clad in a livery of green, with bows in their hands and about a hundred noblemen on horseback all gorgeously arrayed'.

Records show that May games were played in Fenchurch Street, London, on May 30, 1557 – and it seems that May celebrations sometimes extended past May. In 1555, for example, on June 3, there was 'a goodly May-gam at Westmynster' with dancing, music and other merriment. A few years later, in 1559, as part of the celebrations, people piled into boats opposite the palace at Westminster to pelt each other with eggs and oranges! Some set fire to squibs (small fireworks); unfortunately one landed in a barrel of gunpowder, which exploded, and one person was drowned.

The Puritan government under Oliver Cromwell banned May celebrations and maypoles, but they made a welcome return after the Restoration; Pepys noted the maypole in the Strand in his diary in 1663. His entry for May 28, 1667, related that his wife went to Woolwich with two companions '… in order to take a little ayre and to lie there to-morrow and so to gather May dew tomorrow morning, which Mrs. Turner hath taught her is the only thing in the world to wash her face with, and I am contented with it'.

At Greenwich, young couples rolled down Greenwich Hill at the yearly fair. The annual May Fair was moved to Brookfield Westminster, next to Piccadilly in 1688, and lasted for a fortnight. Evidently some people regarded it as a great nuisance; a pamphlet was issued in 1709 calling for its closure because the booths were not 'for trade and merchandise, but for musicke, shows, drinking, raffling, lotteries, stage-plays and drolls'.

> *To Islington and Hogsdon runnes the streame*
> *Of giddie people, to eat cakes and creame.*

Traditional foods included milky puddings, creamy desserts and cheesecakes made with soft cream cheese. Hasty pudding, a blancmange-like pudding was especially well-liked in Ireland, particularly by children. As the name suggests, it could be made ready with very little notice.

In medieval England, particularly in the Yorkshire Dales, enormous flocks of sheep owned by the monasteries grazed on the lush pastures. Ewes-milk cheeses were common, and to a lesser extent, so were goats cheeses. Hard cheeses made from skimmed milk were an important part of the diet of the poor, although these were not approved of by physicians, and wealthy people avoided them completely, preferring soft cheeses made from cream and rich milk.

Butter and cheese went to the lord of the manor, but the peasants and serfs had the right to the milk of the whole flock for a week after the spring equinox, during which time they could make cheese and butter for their own use during the rest of the year. In order to improve their keeping qualities, both butter and cheese were often salted. Few people drank milk in its raw state, because it was believed to curdle in the stomach. Milk was usually boiled with honey for drinking purposes and boiled with cereal or made into custards with eggs. Curds and whey were eaten regularly, either alone or with honey, ale or wine, according to the wealth or poverty of the consumer.

Curdled milk was also used to make junket, which remained popular up to the eighteenth century, until cream became more affordable by everyone and the more easily made cream-based syllabubs and fools came into vogue.

Milk braised pork

1 tablespoon oil
25g/¼ stick butter
1 x 1kg/2¼ pound piece loin of pork, rind removed
1 onion, chopped
600ml/2½ cups milk
3-4 sprigs fresh sage
Salt and pepper

Heat the oil and butter in a large pan or flameproof casserole dish and cook the pork and onion for 15 minutes, until the pork is browned on all sides.

Pour in the milk. Add the sage and season to taste. Bring to the boil, then cover and simmer for 1¾–2 hours until the pork is tender, turning it occasionally during cooking.

Place the pork on a heated serving dish. Remove the sage from the pan and discard. Liquidize the sauce in a food processor or blender until smooth and pour into a heated sauceboat or jug.

Serve the pork in thick slices accompanied with the sauce.

An unusual but very good method of cooking pork, which results in meltingly tender meat with a delicious flavour.

Rich cheese fritters

50g/2 ounces flour
200ml/1 cup double (heavy) cream
4 eggs
115/4 ounces mature Cheddar cheese, grated
50g/½ stick butter
Freshly grated nutmeg
Pinch ground mace (optional)
1 teaspoon salt
1 teaspoon pepper
Oil for frying

Whisk the flour into the cream in a pan. Bring to the boil, whisking all the time, then remove from the heat and cool slightly.

Whisk the eggs until frothy and beat into the cooled cream. Stir in the remaining ingredients and beat until well mixed.

Heat the oil in a deep frying pan. Drop tablespoons of the batter into the hot oil and cook for about 1 minute each side until golden and puffy. Drain on kitchen paper (paper towels) and serve hot.

These crisp, golden puffs are made with cream and were very popular in the eighteenth century.

Cheese cutlets

(Bradford Family Recipe)

115g/4 ounces mature Cheddar cheese, grated
25g/¼ stick butter
2 eggs
Pinch cayenne pepper
1 teaspoon prepared mustard
1 tablespoon double (heavy) cream
Dried breadcrumbs to coat
Oil for frying
Parsley to garnish

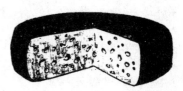

Beat the cheese with the butter until well combined. Beat in one egg, cayenne and mustard and add just enough cream to bind the mixture. Chill in the fridge to firm up.

Shape the mixture into 6-8 cutlets. Beat the remaining egg and dip the cutlets into the egg and toss in the breadcrumbs until well-coated.

Heat the oil and when hot, cook the cutlets until crisp and golden. Serve immediately garnished with parsley. Crisp and golden on the outside and oozing soft melted cheese on the inside, these go well with a crisp green salad.

Not exactly a suitable recipe for the dieting fraternity, and, even worse,
extremely more-ish, but so much more fun than just eating a piece of cheese.
This is not something I have ever seen served anywhere else; I assume it was an
invention of my mother's. It was definitely always a popular family favourite.
   It is also very suitable as an option for vegetarians, as long as you use
Cheddar that has not been made by using rennet. RB

Wensleydale pudding

115g/4 ounces Wensleydale cheese, crumbled (use very young Cheddar or even feta if Wensleydale isn't available)
50g/2 ounces fresh white breadcrumbs
2 eggs
450ml/2¼ cups milk
Salt and pepper
A little freshly grated nutmeg

Preheat the oven to 180°C/350°F/gas mark 4. Butter a 900ml/ approximately 1-quart baking dish.

Put all the ingredients into a mixing bowl and mix well. Pour into the dish and cook for 30 minutes until golden and puffy. Serve hot with green vegetables or a crisp green salad.

An old-fashioned supper dish that's deliciously light and airy – similar to a soufflé.

Cheese and ale

*675g/1½ pounds Cheshire cheese (use mild Cheddar or Colby if
Cheshire is unavailable)*
250ml/1⅛ cups strong dark ale
1 tablespoon prepared English mustard
Cayenne pepper
Pinch of freshly grated nutmeg
Freshly toasted bread

Slice the cheese very thinly and put into
a heavy pan along with the ale. Heat until
the mixture is bubbling. Reduce the heat and
cook, stirring until all the cheese has melted.

Add the mustard and stir until smooth. Remove from the heat
and stir in the cayenne and nutmeg.

Lay the toast on warm plates and spoon the cheese mixture on
top. Serve immediately.

*This tasty old English dish was often served to travellers in the area in local
inns and taverns.*

Rich cheese tart

250g/9 ounces shortcrust (medium-flake) pastry
200g/7 ounces cheese, grated or finely chopped
200ml/⅞ cup double (heavy) cream
4 eggs, beaten
Large pinch of freshly grated nutmeg
Salt (depending on the saltiness of the cheese) and pepper to taste

Preheat the oven to 200°C/400°F/gas mark 6. Grease a 25-28cm/ 10-11-inch flan tin or pie dish.

Roll out the pastry on a floured surface about 3mm/⅛ inch thick and line the flan tin. Bake for 12 minutes. Remove from the oven and reduce the oven temperature to 190°C/375°F/gas mark 5.

Combine the remaining ingredients, mixing well until thoroughly blended and turn into the pastry case. Cook for 30-45 minutes until the mixture has set and the surface is browned; if it's browning too quickly, cover with foil.

Remove from the oven and leave to cool and firm up for 5-10 minutes. Serve immediately.

You can use any cheese for this tasty tart, e.g. Cheddar, Cheshire, Double Gloucester, etc. You can also use a soft, rich cheese, in which case use just over half the quantity given in the recipe.

Cambridge burnt cream tart

175g/6 ounces shortcrust (medium-flake) pastry
250ml/1⅛ cups double or whipping cream
4 egg yolks
2 tablespoons caster (superfine) sugar
1 teaspoon vanilla extract
4 tablespoons icing (confectioner's) sugar

Preheat the oven to 190°C/375°F/gas mark 5. Grease a shallow loose-based 20cm/8-inch flan tin or pie dish.

Roll out the pastry and line the tin. Bake blind for 10 minutes, then remove the baking beans and paper and cook for another 5-10 minutes. Remove from the oven and reduce the oven temperature to 120°C/225°F/gas mark ¼.

Bring the cream to the boil in a pan and immediately remove from the heat.

Whisk the egg yolks with the sugar in a bowl, then slowly pour on the hot cream and add the vanilla. Strain the mixture into the pastry case and bake for about 45 minutes, or until the filling has set. Leave the tart to cool completely.

Preheat the grill (broiler) to medium and sprinkle the top of the tart with the icing sugar. Protect the pastry with foil. Place under the grill until the top is brown and bubbling. Cool before serving.

Cambridge burnt cream was served at Cambridge University as part of the May week celebrations. Here the silky-smooth, creamy filling is baked in a crisp pastry shell.

Hasty pudding

600ml/2½ cups milk
50g/2 ounces plain (all-purpose) flour
25g/¼ stick butter
2 tablespoons sugar
3 eggs
Few drops vanilla extract
1 teaspoon ground cinnamon, optional

Preheat the oven to 180°C/350°F/gas mark 4. Butter a medium pie dish.

Pour almost all the milk into a pan and bring to the boil. Mix the remaining milk with the flour in a bowl until smooth. Pour on the boiling milk, stirring constantly. Pour back into the pan and bring to the boil, stirring. Simmer for 2 minutes until smooth and thick.

Remove from the heat and stir in the butter and sugar; leave to cool. Stir in the eggs and vanilla, then add the cinnamon if using.

Put into the prepared dish and bake for 30 minutes. Serve hot with whipped cream, jam or preserves, treacle (molasses) or honey.

The ingredients of this pudding vary according to the area, but in general it was a sweet milk pudding made with flour, oatmeal, semolina or tapioca. In its most basic form, the cereal and milk were boiled and served immediately with butter and sugar. Richer, tastier versions added butter and eggs to the basic ingredients, and the mixture was baked after boiling. The pudding was served with black treacle (molasses) and/or fresh thick cream.

Cream custard cake

1 egg and 4 egg yolks
200g/2 sticks unsalted butter, softened
225g/8 ounces caster (superfine) sugar
Pinch of salt
Finely grated zest of 1 lemon
350g/12 ounces plain (all-purpose) flour
150ml/⅝ cup milk
150ml/⅝ cup single (light) cream

Preheat the oven to 200°C/400°F/gas mark 6. Butter a shallow
23cm/9-inch round cake tin (pan).

Beat the whole egg with 2 egg yolks, then beat in the butter,
200g/7 ounces of sugar, salt, lemon zest and 325g/11½ ounces
flour until smooth and shiny. Leave to stand for 1 hour.

Meanwhile, beat the remaining sugar and flour together with 2
egg yolks in a pan until smooth. Add the milk and cream and stir
over a low heat until thick. Allow to cool.

Put two-thirds of the cake mixture into the prepared tin and cover
with the custard. Top with the remaining cake mixture. Bake for
30-40 minutes, or until the cake is cooked. Cool in the tin before
removing carefully to a serving plate.

It's essential to use butter in this recipe to ensure the best flavour and a rich
moist texture in this delectable cake.

Honey syllabub

3 tablespoons brandy
3 tablespoons sherry or white wine
600ml/2½ cups double (heavy) cream
6 tablespoons honey
30g/1 ounce flaked almonds
Sponge fingers (or lady fingers) to serve

Combine the brandy and sherry or white wine. Place the cream in a chilled bowl and whisk until just thickened. Add the honey and whisk again for about 15 seconds.

Pour the brandy and sherry in a continuous stream onto the cream and honey, whisking all the time until the liquid is absorbed and the mixture forms soft peaks.

Spoon into serving glasses and chill for 2-3 hours. Just before serving, sprinkle with the almonds and place 2 sponge fingers or lady fingers on the side of each dish.

Light and luscious syllabub has a long history: it was a favourite of both Elizabeth I and Charles II. You can use any honey; the distinctive taste of heather honey is especially good.

Sack posset

600ml/2½ cups single (light) cream
1-2 tablespoons caster (superfine) sugar
2 egg yolks
Grated rind of 1 small lemon
3 tablespoons dry white wine

Put the cream and sugar into a pan and
heat gently to simmering point; don't
allow to boil.

Whisk the egg yolks in a bowl and pour on the hot cream,
whisking all the time. Whisk in the lemon rind and wine.

Place the bowl over a pan of simmering (not boiling) water and
stir until the mixture thickens and coats the back of a spoon.

Cool slightly then pour into 4 serving dishes and leave to cool.
Chill before serving.

*A delicate wine-flavoured cream custard that was extremely popular in
England in the eighteenth century.*

Geranium cream

300ml/1¼ cups double (heavy) cream
75g/3 ounces sugar
3-4 geranium leaves
175g/6 ounces soft cream cheese

Heat the cream, sugar and geranium leaves slowly in a pan over a low heat until the cream is hot but not boiling. Remove from the heat, cover and leave until cold.

Gradually beat the cold cream mixture into the cream cheese until smooth and creamy. Cover and leave to stand in a cool place (not the refrigerator) for 12 hours.

Remove the leaves and spoon the mixture into serving dishes. Serve with whipped cream and summer fruits.

Strongly scented geranium leaves impart a wonderful fragrance to this creamy dessert. You can use either lemon or rose geranium leaves.

Gooseberries and cream ice cream

500g/generous 1 pound gooseberries, topped and tailed
2 tablespoons Muscat wine
115g/4 ounces sugar (you may need more if the berries are very tart)
225ml/1 cup whipping cream

Put the gooseberries in a pan with the wine and sugar. Heat
gently until the sugar has dissolved and simmer for about 5-10
minutes, or until soft. Tip into a food processor or blender and
process to a purée. Sieve to remove the pips and skins. Cool, and
then chill in the refrigerator.

Whip the cream until thick (but not stiff) and fold into the cold
purée until well combined. Churn in an ice-cream maker.
Alternatively place in a freezer-proof container and freeze until
half-frozen, remove from the freezer and tip into a bowl, whisk
vigorously to break down any ice crystals, return to the freezer
and repeat the process once more.

Place in the refrigerator 30 minutes before serving.

Gooseberry-growing was all the rage in nineteenth-century Lancashire,
Cheshire, Yorkshire, Derbyshire and Staffordshire, and special clubs were
formed by the growers. Annual gooseberry shows (held in England since 1809)
are still popular events in these regions. Competitors bring their prized berries
to the show in sealed boxes and the various competitions begin to find the
heaviest berry, the juiciest and those with the best colour.

WHIT BANK HOLIDAY

The UK's modern 'spring bank holiday' – a Monday off work in May – was known in the past as Whitsuntide and celebrated the feast of Pentecost: the gift of the Holy Spirit to the apostles in the form of 'a violent wind and tongues of fire' 50 days after Easter (*penteconta* means 50 in Greek). The origin of the word 'Whitsuntide' is lost in time, but a fourteenth-century rhyme offers a clue:

> *This day Whitsun is cald*
> *For wisdom and wit sevenfold*
> *Was goven to the apostles on this day.*

The name may also be due to the white robes that were worn on the Sunday by those about to be baptized, as Pentecost was a popular time for baptisms in the past.

The Whitsuntide festivities of the past have their origins in the love feasts of the early Christians, and the 'drinklean': an annual festival of the tenants and vassals of the feudal lords. They became known as 'Whitsun ales' because the church wardens laid in a stock of malt, which they brewed into beer and sold for refreshment in the church porch or, more usually, in the churchyard. The proceeds of these sales were given to the poor.

Whitsun was a time for village feasts, games, picnics and walks. Everyone dressed in their best clothes, and after church services and walks, would meet on the village green for an enormous communal feast of cold meats, baked hams, pies, custards and fruit tarts, a custom which lasted into the twentieth century. A special 'love feast cake' was always included: a rich fruit cake that could be made ahead as it kept well and was easy to transport. Whit Monday fairs were held in every town and were enormously popular. Cakes and sweetmeats unique to each region were sold at the fairs and while some of these regional delicacies have died out, a few have become universal favourites.

The town of Oldbury in Gloucestershire was renowned for the delicious gooseberry tarts which followed the traditional roast ox at the Whitsun feast. The 'tarts' were in fact little pies made with hot-water-crust pastry (as used to make pork pies), which made them crisp and golden on the outside, while the inside was softened by the sugary juices from the fruit.

Goosenargh cakes, a speciality of the Lancashire town of Preston, were actually biscuits (cookies) with a thick, sugary crust flavoured with coriander or caraway seeds, and were baked in great quantities for Whit. People flocked to the town to enjoy the cakes, and it was once estimated that about 50,000 were sold annually.

In Kingsteignton in Devon it was the custom on Whit Monday for a live ram to be pulled through the streets on a cart decorated with laburnum and lilac garlands. Everyone was expected to contribute towards the cost of the ceremony. The ram was roasted the next day and slices of the meat were sold cheaply to the poor.

Cheesecakes were also great favourites at Whit Monday feasts and fairs and were ideal for using the surplus curds produced by sour milk. Cows produced their maximum yield of milk in May, but the warm summer weather meant that it was impossible to keep spare milk for any length of time, so surplus milk was turned into cream, butter and cheese, with some being kept aside to make delectably rich cakes and puddings. Cheese mentioned in medieval recipes was invariably a soft cheese known as 'ruayn', which was used to make cheesecakes and tarts for the nobility. Anne Boleyn was said to have been particularly fond of cheesecake.

A Gloucestershire speciality that was specially made for Whitsuntide was 'white pot' or 'white pont', an unusual sweet pudding made from milk, flour, black treacle (molasses) and spices. Cold water was added just before the pudding was baked and formed a white jelly in the centre. The pudding was baked in a deep dish in a farmhouse bread oven and firmed up as it cooled. It was eaten warm or cold.

The famous contest for the Dunmow Flitch, which still takes place on Whit Monday at Dunmow in Essex, is said to date back to 1104. Chaucer alludes to the Dunmow Flitch Trials in 'The Wife of Bath's Tale'. To claim the flitch (side) of bacon, a married couple had to kneel in the churchyard and swear before the townspeople and priest that they had never quarrelled or regretted their marriage. Since the end of the Second World War, the contest has been held every four years in a leap year. A court presided over by a judge has counsel representing the claimants, and opposing counsel representing the donors of the flitch of bacon, a jury of six maidens and six bachelors, a clerk of the court and an usher. The court is held in a marquee erected on Talberds Ley especially for the occasion, and couples married for at least a year and a day come from near and far to try and claim the flitch.

It is not a competition between the couples; all couples could be successful in their claim, which is vigorously defended by counsel employed on behalf of the donors of the bacon, whose job it is to test their evidence and to try and persuade the jury not to grant them the flitch. Successful couples are then carried shoulder-high by bearers in the ancient flitch chair to the market-place where they take an oath (similar to pre-Reformation marriage vows) kneeling on pointed stones. Unsuccessful couples have to walk behind the empty chair to the market-place, although they have the consolation of winning a prize of gammon (ham).

Crowds of people still flock to Dunmow to celebrate this tradition. The saying 'to bring home the bacon', (meaning to prove your worth) is believed to come from these trials.

Spicy salmon in pastry

1 whole salmon, boned and cleaned but with head and tail left on
Salt and pepper
3-4 teaspoons ground cumin
3-4 teaspoons chilli powder
1 teaspoon paprika
Juice of 1 lemon
50g/½ stick butter, diced
450g/1 pound shortcrust (medium-flake) pastry
1 raisin or currant (for the 'eye')
1 egg white beaten with 1 tablespoon cream

Preheat the oven to 200°C/400°F/gas mark 6. Line a large baking tray or roasting tin (pan) with non-stick paper.

Season the inside of the fish with salt and pepper and sprinkle with the spices and lemon juice. Insert the pieces of butter into the fish.

Roll out the pastry in an oval shape 5cm/2 inches longer than the fish at each end, ensuring that it is wide enough to enclose the fish, allowing for sealing the pastry edges. Gently lift the fish onto the pastry and fold the pastry over. Trim off any excess. Dampen the edges with water and press well to seal.

Carefully place the parcel onto a baking tray. Cut out oval 'scales' from the pastry trimmings and stick them on with water, overlapping them. Stick on the raisin for the 'eye'. Very gently brush the pastry with the egg white and cream mixture.

Bake for 10 minutes then reduce the temperature to 180°C/350°F/gas mark 4 and cook another 20-30 minutes, according to the thickness and size of the salmon. Serve hot or cold.

An ideal dish for a special summer picnic. The word 'picnic' was first used around 1740 and was probably derived from the French verb piquer *(to pick at food) and* nique *(something small of no value).*

Salmon tartare

300g/10½ ounces salmon fillets, skinned and cubed

For the marinade
1 tablespoon Thai fish sauce
4 tablespoons lime juice
2 teaspoons strong-flavoured honey, e.g. chestnut
1 small chilli (seeds removed), finely chopped
1 clove of garlic, crushed
Pinch of salt
Handful of coriander (cilantro) leaves
4 spring onions, sliced diagonally
Sesame seeds for sprinkling

Combine all the marinade ingredients in a bowl. Add the trout and stir well. Cover and chill for up to 8 hours, stirring occasionally.

Drain off the marinade. Toss the fish with the coriander leaves and spring onions. Place on a plate and sprinkle with the sesame seeds. Serve with a crisp green salad and new potatoes.

You can also use trout fillets for this delicious summer dish.

Vegetable frittata

2 tablespoons oil
1 onion, chopped
3 courgettes (zucchini), finely sliced
6 large eggs
Salt and freshly ground black pepper

Heat the oil in a frying pan, add the onion and cook for 2 minutes, until soft.

Add the courgettes (zucchini) and fry for 4 minutes, until golden.

Beat the eggs with the salt and pepper. Pour the eggs into the pan and cook for about 10 minutes.

Place the pan under a hot grill (broiler) for a few minutes until the top is browned. Stand for 10 minutes, then turn out and leave to cool.

Serve cold cut into wedges with a green salad.

A deliciously thick, solid omelette that looks impressive accompanied by a fresh green salad.

Picnic loaf

1 large round rustic loaf
2 large tomatoes
2 tablespoons fruity olive oil
175g/6 ounces cooked ham, sliced
½ crisp lettuce, shredded
3 tablespoons mayonnaise
115g/4 ounces cheese, cubed
Few black olives (optional)
Salt and pepper

Slice the top off the loaf and scoop out the centre, leaving a 'shell' about 2.5cm/1 inch thick. You can freeze the breadcrumbs for later use.

Sprinkle the inside of the bread case with oil and season to taste.

Slice the tomatoes and layer with the ham and lettuce in the bread case. Season to taste, spread with mayonnaise and scatter over the cheese and olives.

Cover with the bread lid and wrap tightly in foil. Chill until needed and cut in wedges to serve.

A rustic bread loaf that's far nicer than soggy sandwiches. You can vary the ingredients according to taste.

Ham baked with cider and rosemary

1½-2kg/3-4½ pounds boned and rolled gammon (ham) joint
1 onion, quartered
1 stick celery, sliced
5 cloves
Parsley stalks
2 bay leaves
Few sprigs fresh rosemary
100g/3½ ounces demerara (light brown cane) sugar
100g/3½ ounces Dijon mustard
300ml/1¼ cups dry cider (applejack)

Soak the gammon in cold water if necessary; this isn't always
needed so check with your supplier or with the instructions on
the pack. Place the gammon in a large pan, cover with cold water
and bring to the boil. Skim off any scum that rises to the top.
Add the onion, celery, cloves, parsley, bay leaves and rosemary.
Cover and slowly simmer for 1½ hours.

When cooked, place the meat in a roasting tin (pan) and remove
the skin, leaving the fat intact. Score the fat into diamond shapes.
Pour half the cider into the roasting tin.

Preheat the oven to 220°C/425°F/gas mark 7. Mix the sugar with
just enough mustard to make a paste. Brush over the scored fat
and bake for 35-40 minutes. Mix the remaining mustard and cider
and baste the ham several times during cooking. When the fat is
golden, transfer to a warm plate and
leave until cold before slicing.

A moist, succulent ham makes an
elegant centrepiece for a sophisticated
al fresco *meal.*

Cold spiced chicken

6 chicken legs or 12 chicken drumsticks

For the marinade
1 teaspoon freshly ground black pepper
½ teaspoon ground cumin
½ teaspoon ground cinnamon
1 teaspoon ground ginger
4 teaspoons honey
2 teaspoons paprika
2 cloves garlic, crushed
Pinch of salt
3 tablespoons olive oil

For the salad
Crisp lettuce leaves
1 cucumber, cut into strips
4 spring onions, trimmed
2 lemons, quartered

Score the chicken pieces deeply with a sharp knife. Combine the marinade ingredients in a bowl. Turn the chicken pieces in the mixture and leave to marinate for at least 2 hours or overnight.

Preheat a moderate grill (broiler) and cook the chicken for 20 minutes, turning once. Leave until cold, then wrap in greaseproof (waxed) paper and foil.

Combine the salad ingredients and transfer to an airtight container. Serve the chicken with the salad.

Ideal for a picnic. Pack the chicken and salad in a well-insulated cool-box to keep them chilled and fresh.

Oldbury tarts

225ml/1 cup boiling water
75g/¾ stick butter
75g/3 ounces lard
450g/1 pound plain (all-purpose) flour
1 tablespoon icing (confectioner's) sugar
400g/14 ounces small green gooseberries
50g/2 ounces caster (superfine) sugar

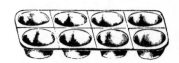

Preheat the oven to 200°C/400°F/gas mark 6. Grease 12-15-hole patty or bun tins (cupcake pans).

Mix the boiling water with the butter and lard, stirring until the fats have melted. Sift the flour and icing sugar into a mixing bowl and pour in the liquid. Mix to a pliable dough, knead for a minute and allow to cool slightly.

Roll out the dough on a lightly floured surface about .5cm/¼ inch thick. Cut into 12-15 rounds with a 7.5cm/3-inch cutter and another 12-15 rounds using a 6cm/2½-inch cutter. Line the tins with the larger rounds.

Fill the cases with the gooseberries, sprinkling a little of the sugar over the fruit. Dampen the edges of the smaller rounds with water and cover the tarts, pressing the edges well to seal. Cut a slit in the top of each pie to allow the steam to escape. Bake for 15-20 minutes until golden brown.

Serve warm or cold with custard, cream or ice cream

If you are used to handling hot-water-crust pastry, the dough can be moulded by hand. Adding icing sugar to the dough produces a crisper pastry.

Revel buns

½ teaspoon saffron strands
3 tablespoons warm milk
225g/8 ounces strong plain (all-purpose) flour
Pinch of salt
½ teaspoon ground cinnamon
55g/½ stick butter
55g/2 ounces currants
25g/1 ounce fresh yeast
1 teaspoon sugar
2-3 tablespoons thick double (heavy) or clotted cream
1 egg, beaten

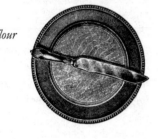

Stir the saffron into the warm milk, cover and leave to stand for a few hours or overnight.

Sift the flour, salt and cinnamon into a mixing bowl and rub in the butter until the mixture resembles breadcrumbs. Add the currants and make a well in the centre. Reheat the saffron milk until warm but not hot. Cream the yeast and sugar and leave for a few minutes until frothy, then gradually add the saffron milk, cream and almost all the egg. Pour into the well and mix to a soft dough.

Turn out onto a floured surface and knead for 2-3 minutes. Return to the bowl, cover and leave in a warm place until doubled in size. Divide into 8 pieces and shape each into a round bun. Place on a greased baking sheet, cover and leave in a warm place for 20 minutes.

Preheat the oven to 190°C/375°F/gas mark 5. Grease a large baking tray. Brush the tops of the buns lightly with the remaining egg and bake for 15-20 minutes until golden brown. Cool on a wire rack.

These golden yellow buns were made in the West Country for the Whitsun festivities (revels) held on Whit Sunday and Whit Monday.

Whitsun cake

375g/13 ounces strong white bread flour
Pinch of salt
75g/¾ stick butter
15g/½ ounce fresh yeast
150ml/⅛ cup warm milk
115g/1 stick butter, melted
225g/8 ounces raisins
225g/8 ounces sugar
Pinch of grated nutmeg
Pinch ground cinnamon
1 egg, separated

Sift the flour and salt into a mixing bowl and rub in the butter.
Crumble the yeast into the milk and leave until frothy, then add to
the flour with 75g/¾ stick melted butter. Knead to a soft dough,
then cover and leave to rise for 45 minutes.

Meanwhile, mix the raisins, sugar and spices with the remaining
melted butter in a pan and simmer gently for 10 minutes. Leave
to cool, then beat in the egg yolk.

Preheat the oven to 200°C/400°F/gas mark 6. Grease a 20cm/
8-inch round cake tin (pan).

Divide the dough into 4 pieces and roll out to fit the base of the
cake tin. Place one round of dough in the tin and top with a third
of the raisin mixture. Repeat twice and top with the remaining
dough. Seal the edges firmly with a little egg white. Bake for 45
minutes, then brush with the rest of the egg white and return to
the oven for another 10 minutes.

Turn out onto a wire rack to cool. Keep in an airtight tin for 2
days before eating to allow the filling to flavour the dough layers.

A rich speciality from Lincolnshire, made specially for Whitsuntide festivities.

Summer fruit cheesecake

For the base
150g/5½ ounces digestive biscuits (graham crackers)
50g/½ stick butter, melted
25g/1 ounce sugar

2 x 200g/7-ounce tubs soft cheese
Finely grated zest and juice of 1 small lemon
3 eggs separated
115g/4 ounces icing (confectioner's) sugar
25g/1 ounce plain (all-purpose) flour

For the topping
350g/12 ounces raspberries and halved strawberries
50g/2 ounces demerara (light brown cane) sugar

Preheat the oven to 180°C/350°F/gas mark 4. Grease a 20cm/
8-inch springform cake tin (pan).

Place the biscuits in a plastic bag and crush with a rolling pin. Stir
the crumbs into the melted butter with the sugar. Press into the
base of the prepared tin and chill.

Whisk the cheese, lemon zest and juice, egg yolks and golden icing
sugar in a large bowl until smooth. Whisk the egg whites until just
stiff, then fold into mixture with the sifted flour. Pour into the tin
and bake for about 55 minutes until firm. Switch off the oven and
leave to cool; this stops the cheesecake from sinking.

Preheat the grill (broiler) to high. When cold, remove from the tin
and transfer to a heatproof serving plate. Arrange the prepared
fruits on top of the cheesecake. Sprinkle with the demerara sugar
and grill for 2-3 minutes until the sugar caramelizes.

A modern recipe topped with delicious seasonal fruits.

Floating islands

8 egg whites
Pinch salt
8 tablespoons caster (superfine) sugar
600ml/2½ cups milk
600ml/2½ cups double (heavy) cream
1 vanilla pod
8 egg yolks
225g/8 ounces sugar

Whisk the egg whites and salt until stiff, then gradually beat in the caster sugar.

Heat the milk in a large frying pan and when simmering, place tablespoons of the meringue mixture on top. Poach for 2 minutes on each side, turning once. Remove with a perforated spoon and place on kitchen paper (paper towels) to dry.

Pour the warm milk and cream into a pan with the vanilla pod. Beat the egg yolks with the caster sugar and whisk into the milk and cream. Pour the mixture into a bowl and place over a pan of simmering (not boiling) water. Stir constantly until the mixture thickens enough to coat the back of the spoon. Pour into a large bowl, cover the top with greaseproof (waxed) paper to stop a skin forming on the custard, and leave to cool.

Arrange the poached meringues on top of the custard.
Serve immediately.

A very pretty dessert: light, airy poached meringues floating on a 'sea' of sweetened, creamy custard. Be careful not to overcook the meringues or they will break up.

Gooseberry fool

675g/1½ pounds green gooseberries, topped and tailed
150ml/⅝ cup water
175g/6 ounces caster (superfine) sugar

For the custard
300ml/1¼ cups single (light) cream
1 teaspoon cornflour (cornstarch)
2 tablespoons caster (superfine) sugar
4 egg yolks
150ml/⅝ cup double (heavy) cream

Put the gooseberries into a pan with the water and sugar and simmer until soft and pulpy. Push through a sieve (or blend in a food processor or liquidizer before sieving) and leave to cool.

Mix 2 tablespoons single cream with the cornflour and sugar in a bowl. Bring the rest of the single cream to the boil and pour onto the cornflour mixture, stirring. Return to the pan and beat in the egg yolks. Cook over a very low heat until the custard is thick and smooth. Leave to cool.

Combine the cooled custard with the gooseberry purée. Whisk the double cream until thick but not stiff and gently fold into the fruit mixture a little at a time. Beat until light and spoon into serving dishes. Chill before serving.

Fools were a favourite dessert in Tudor times.
The name comes from the French fouler, *'to mash'. In its early days the dish was a blend of cream, mashed fruit, sugar and sometimes spices.*

Clotted cream ice cream

375ml/1⅝ cups creamy milk
125g/4½ ounces caster (superfine) sugar
5 egg yolks
125ml/½ cup clotted cream (use crème fraîche if not available)
Few drops vanilla essence

Put the milk and half the sugar in a pan and heat gently until the sugar has dissolved. Heat until almost boiling.

Beat the egg yolks with the rest of the sugar until thick and pale. Pour the hot milk in a steady stream onto the egg yolks, whisking all the time. Place the bowl over a pan of simmering (not boiling) water and cook, stirring, until thick enough to coat the back of a wooden spoon. Remove from the heat and leave to cool.

Stir in the clotted cream and vanilla and leave until cold. Pour into a freezer-proof container, cover and freeze until firm. Place in the refrigerator to soften slightly 20 minutes before serving.

Gloriously yellow clotted cream is lusciously thick and rich with a minimum fat content of 55 percent. It is particularly associated with West County cream teas. It makes a sumptuously rich ice cream.

White pot

115g/4 ounces plain (all-purpose) flour
½ teaspoon ground mixed spice
¼ teaspoon freshly grated nutmeg
115g/½ cup black treacle or molasses
2 eggs, beaten
1.1 litre/1 generous quart milk
25g/¼ stick butter
75ml/generous ¼ cup cold water

Preheat the oven to 180°C/350°F/gas mark 4. Butter a deep baking dish.

Sift the flour and spices into a mixing bowl and stir in the treacle. Beat in the eggs and a little of the milk.

Heat the rest of the milk in a pan until boiling and pour into the flour mixture, stirring well. Turn the mixture into the prepared dish and dot with the butter. Pour the cold water into the middle of the dish but do not stir.

Bake for 1 hour, or until the pudding has separated into a jelly at the base and a custard on top. Serve hot or cold.

Other additions to the ingredients might include dried fruits, sugar or breadcrumbs.

MIDSUMMER

The Feast of St John the Baptist falls on June 24, which was once celebrated as Midsummer's Day and regarded as an important date in the calendar. Certain flowers and herbs considered to have magic properties were gathered and woven into garlands to be worn on the head or around the neck and were also placed around the necks of farm animals to ward off evil spirits. St John's wort was considered especially important, and the yellow herb was commonly known in country areas as 'chase-the-devil', because it was widely believed that it had the power to ward off the devil and also to cure many ailments. A sprig was often placed over the doorway of a house as a protection.

The night before Midsummer's Day was called St John's Eve, when it was the custom to light bonfires at midnight. A sixteenth-century poem contained the lines:

> *Then doth the joyful feast of St John the Baptist take his turn*
> *When bonfires great with lofty flame*
> *in every town do burn*

People danced round the fires, and when the flames had died down they would jump over them to ensure good luck and protection from evil. It was also customary for people to fast and to keep vigil throughout the night in the porch of the local church, in the belief that they would see the spectres of those in the parish who would die during the coming year.

Summer has always been a busy time for sheep farmers. Until fairly recently sheep had to be clipped of their heavy winter fleeces by hand, and it was also the traditional time for haymaking and making cheese and butter. In the sheep-rearing English county of Cumbria, clipping the sheep was a communal event and the clippers met at each farm in turn so that each flock could be clipped in a single day. Until the mid-nineteenth century the clipping ended with a barefoot race for a fleece mounted on a pole.

Farmers' wives took charge of feeding the farm labourers and their families and provided huge communal meals that were occasions for celebration as well as for enjoying good food. Everyone stopped work at 7pm and gathered in the farmhouse – or outside if the weather was fine – for a lavish supper of joints of meat, pies, cheeses, homemade bread, pickles and relishes, cakes, tarts and puddings. Clipping time suppers were eagerly anticipated, especially by the local children, as they were happy, fun-filled events with singing and dancing.

Clipping time pudding featured at the meal and was a particular favourite in the Lake District. A type of rice pudding, it often had to be cooked in the local baker's oven if the baking dish was too big to fit into a farmhouse oven. The pudding contained dried fruits and spices and was enriched with bone marrow and eggs. It was cooked slowly for a long time to produce a rich, creamy pudding which was eaten alone or with cream. Clipping time celebrations died out during the First World War.

One of the oldest midsummer treats is a bowl of the new season's strawberries. Wild strawberries have been enjoyed for thousands of years, and as early as the tenth century, the luscious scarlet berries were eagerly sought out in woods and undergrowth. It wasn't until around 1300 that wild strawberry plants were transplanted into cottage gardens and smallholdings and their cultivation became widespread; the fruit became known as the 'straeberie'. Quite how the name originated is unclear; it could be because the berries were threaded on straws of grass to make it easier to carry them to market, or it may be derived from the Saxon *streoberie* or *streawberige*, so-called because the plant's runners stray away in all directions. It could also be a corruption of 'strewberry', due to the fact that the berries are strewn among the leaves of the plant, or the fact that straw was placed around the fruiting plants to protect them from frost.

Highly prized strawberries were served at important banquets and feasts. In the Middle Ages the berries symbolized perfection and purity, and the Virgin Mary was often depicted in art with strawberries. Stonemasons of the time carved strawberry designs on altars and stone pillars of churches and cathedrals.

Summer also heralds the appearance of other luscious fruits, such as velvety raspberries and downy-skinned peaches. Peach trees were planted in the royal gardens at Westminster in the thirteenth century, and the fruit was served at important feasts. In the eighteenth century, ovens were built behind the garden walls of the wealthy to supplement the sun's heat; later in the same century hollow walls with flues, heated by furnaces below the ground, provided a more efficient way of keeping in heat, allowing all kinds of delicate and exotic fruits to be grown. Recipes began to appear for 'brandy fruits', and fruits such as peaches were put into jars with brandy and sugar before the jar was sealed tightly.

Sweetly scented edible summer flowers were used in salads, sweetmeats and preserves. The pretty petals added a touch of colour when scattered over a green salad and were also used in stuffings ('forcemeats') for meat and fish. The head chef of Charles II of England had a recipe for cowslip tart: a large handful of the flowers was pounded in a mortar and stirred into a pint of cream. The mixture was scalded over a low heat, then allowed to cool before beating with six eggs, sugar and a little rose-water. After pouring into a pastry shell, the tart was baked in a low oven until set. Cowslips possess sedative properties and were made into wines and syrups which were sipped before bedtime to ensure a good night's sleep.

Cool, creamy ice cream is a delicious treat on a hot summer's day. Ice cream was first made in Britain in the eighteenth century from fresh cream, sugar and puréed fresh fruits such as peaches or strawberries. Fresh, homemade ice cream is superb; using fresh cream, fruit and other wholesome ingredients gives quite a different flavour and texture to that of commercial ice cream. The added bonus is that ice cream made at home contains no emulsifiers, 'E-numbers' or artificial colouring or flavouring.

Chicken and ham pie

350g/12 ounces shortcrust (medium-flake) pastry
225g/8 ounces pork sausage meat
1 tablespoon chopped thyme
1 large egg, beaten
1kg/2¼ pounds boneless chicken breasts, sliced
450g/1 pound ham, bacon or gammon, sliced
Salt and pepper
3 tablespoons dry white wine
Beaten egg to glaze

For the jellied stock
300ml/1¼ cups chicken stock
2 tablespoons powdered gelatine

Preheat the oven to 220°C/425°F/gas mark 7.

Grease a deep 23cm/9-inch springform cake tin (pan).

Roll out the pastry on a floured surface and use two-thirds to line the prepared tin.

Combine the sausage meat with the thyme and beaten egg. Fill the pastry case with layers of chicken and ham, sprinkling each layer with salt and pepper – be careful if the ham is salty. Spread the sausage meat mixture on top and sprinkle over the wine.

Roll out the remaining pastry and brush the edges with beaten egg. Place on top of the filling and press down to seal the edges well. Brush the top with beaten egg, and cut a slit in the middle.

Bake for 20 minutes to set the pastry, then reduce the heat to 160°C/325°F/gas mark 3 and cook for about 1 hour, or until the meat is cooked. If the pastry is becoming too brown, cover it loosely with foil. Cool the pie in the tin and remove when cold.

To make the jellied stock, pour the stock into a small pan and sprinkle the gelatine on top. Leave for a few minutes to soften, then heat gently until the gelatine has dissolved completely.

When it is on the point of setting, pour into the pie to fill the gaps where the meat has shrunk away from the crust.

Chill until ready to serve.

Pies have always been a cornerstone of English cookery. This tasty, savoury pie with a flavoursome jelly is always served cold.

Cream of pea soup

(Bradford Family Recipe)

15g/½ ounce butter
3 spring onions, finely chopped
1 lettuce, shredded
675g/1½ pounds fresh green peas (shelled weight)
150ml/⅝ cup milk
150ml/⅝ cup single (light) cream
Salt and pepper
½ teaspoon sugar

Heat the butter in a pan and cook the spring
onions and lettuce until the onions are soft
but not browned. Add the peas and just
cover with water. Add the salt, pepper and sugar and bring to the
boil. Reduce the heat and simmer for 20 minutes.

Drain and reserve 150ml/⅝ cup of the cooking liquid. Blend the
vegetables in a food processor or blender (or push through a
sieve) to a purée. Return the mixture to the pan and stir in the
reserved cooking liquor and the milk. Heat through and stir in the
cream but do not allow to boil. Check the seasoning and serve
hot or cold.

*My mother had extremely strong views about peas: very simply, they had to be
picked when they were small and tender, but then we enjoyed the luxury of
fresh produce from a kitchen garden in those days. However, it would not
make much difference where the peas came from here because they are being
combined with other ingredients and then puréed. Most importantly, this
recipe makes the tastiest pea soup I have ever had, and if you want to make
it slightly different, add three or four leaves of mint to the mix. RB*

Strawberry and cucumber salad

2 tablespoons chopped fresh mint
1 teaspoon caster (superfine) sugar
2 tablespoons raspberry or red wine vinegar
4 tablespoons olive oil
Half a cucumber
225g/8 ounces ripe strawberries
White pepper

Place the mint and sugar in a mixing bowl and pound with a wooden spoon to draw out the flavouring oil of the mint. Add the vinegar and oil. Taste the mixture – it should be both sweet and sharp – and add more sugar or vinegar if you wish. Slice the cucumber thinly and stir into the dressing. Cover and marinate until needed.

Slice the strawberries and place on one half of a serving plate. Season lightly with the pepper. Place the cucumber slices on the other half of the plate and spoon over the mint dressing.

This makes an attractive starter for a summer meal. Don't omit the pepper – it really brings out the flavour of the strawberries.

Bacon and egg salad

Approximately 350g/12 ounces mixed salad leaves
Handful of croûtons
4 medium eggs
175g/6 ounces bacon, rind removed and chopped
3 tablespoons white-wine vinegar
Salt and pepper

Arrange the salad leaves on four large plates and scatter with the croûtons.

Gently poach the eggs in a pan of simmering water with a dash of vinegar added. Remove with a slotted spoon and place an egg on top of the greens on each plate.

Fry the bacon without any additional fat until crisp. Drain well and scatter over each salad. Stir the vinegar into the hot bacon fat, season to taste with salt and pepper and spoon over the salads. Serve immediately.

Crisp, refreshing, cool green salad leaves are a welcome addition to summer meals. Full of health-giving minerals and vitamins, salad greens are also low in calories. Choose a selection of leaves of different colours and flavours – mild, bitter, sweet and salty – to add interest and variety.

Green salad with sherry-vinegar dressing

2 teaspoons sherry vinegar
Sea salt and freshly ground black pepper
1 small clove garlic, peeled and finely chopped (optional)
50ml/¼ cup extra-virgin olive oil
200g/7 ounces mixed salad leaves

Whisk together the vinegar, salt and pepper and garlic in a large bowl. Slowly add the oil in a thin stream, whisking constantly until the dressing is emulsified.

Tear the salad leaves into pieces and add to the bowl. Toss well until coated with dressing. Season with salt and pepper if necessary and serve immediately.

Farmers' markets, farm shops and local growers are the best sources of tasty salads. Look for crisp, fresh-looking leaves; if they are limp and droopy or browning at the edges,, they're past their best. To keep lettuce for a couple of days, put the whole unwashed lettuce in a plastic bag, squeeze out the air and seal it tightly. Never cut lettuce, as this bruises the leaves; shred or tear them instead.

Glazed new potatoes

75g/¾ stick butter
75g/3 ounces sugar
1 teaspoon salt
1kg/2¼ pounds cooked small new potatoes
1 tablespoon chopped fresh parsley

Melt the butter and sugar gently in a pan over a low heat until beginning to turn golden brown.

Add the salt and potatoes and toss continuously until they are all well glazed. Sprinkle with the parsley and serve immediately.

Small, waxy potatoes with thin skins are the best to use in this recipe. Around six million tons of potatoes are grown in the UK each year and they are regarded as our national vegetable. Early varieties of new potatoes are available in late spring and early summer, and their superb flavour and texture make them one of the most delicious English vegetables.

Clipping time pudding

115g/4 ounces short-grained rice
Boiling water
1.2 litres/5 cups milk
2.5cm/1-inch piece cinnamon stick (or a good
pinch of ground cinnamon)
Good pinch of freshly grated nutmeg
115g/4 ounces raisins
75g/3 ounces sugar
50g/½ stick butter
1 egg, beaten

Preheat the oven to 170°C/350°F/gas mark 3.

Generously butter a large ovenproof baking dish.

Cover the rice with boiling water and leave to soak for 2 minutes.
Drain the rice and put it into the baking dish along with the rest
of the ingredients. Stir well and cook for 1 hour.

Stir well again and continue cooking for another 1-2 hours, or
until rich and creamy. Serve just as it is or with cream.

The long, slow cooking is essential to form a soft, creamy mass with a rich
brown skin. I've used butter instead of bone marrow, which makes for a
better flavour, but you can use suet instead if you like.

Stawberry tarts

For the pastry
175g/6 ounces plain (all-purpose) flour
Pinch of salt
50g/2 ounces icing (confectioner's) sugar
75g/¾ stick butter, chilled
1 egg yolk mixed with 2 tablespoons cold water

For the filling
300ml/1¼ cups double (heavy) cream
1 tablespoon icing (confectioner's) sugar
1 teaspoon rose-water (optional)
450g/1 pound strawberries, hulled and sliced
4-6 tablespoons redcurrant jelly (use quince if unavailable)

Sift the flour, salt and icing sugar into a mixing bowl and rub in the butter until the mixture resembles breadcrumbs. Add the egg yolk and water and mix to a soft dough. Knead lightly, wrap in cling film (plastic wrap) and chill for 30 minutes.

Preheat the oven to 190°C/375°F/gas mark 5. Roll out the dough thinly, cut into rounds and use it to line bun or tartlet tins (pans). Prick the bases and bake blind for 10-15 minutes until cooked and golden. Leave until completely cold.

Whisk the cream, sugar and rose-water until thick. Spoon into the tarts and top with the strawberries. Melt the redcurrant jelly and brush over the strawberries. Leave to set.

Wash the berries before you hull them. The stem forms a 'plug' which stops the berries becoming waterlogged and soggy.

Strawberry chocolate sponge gateau

50g/2 ounces flaked almonds or chopped hazelnuts
3 large eggs
115g/4 ounces golden caster (golden superfine or baker's) sugar
50g/2 ounces plain (all-purpose) flour
25g/1 ounce cocoa powder
50g/2 ounces ground almonds or hazelnuts

For the filling
350-450g/12 ounces-1 pound strawberries, sliced
300ml/1¼ cups double (heavy) cream, whipped

Preheat the oven to 190°C/375°F/gas mark 5. Grease and line a
30 x 20cm/12 x 8-inch Swiss roll tin (pan).

Toast the flaked almonds or hazelnuts for 5 minutes under a hot
grill (broiler), then leave to cool. Whisk the eggs and sugar with
an electric whisk until very thick and pale. If you don't have an
electric whisk, beat the mixture in a bowl placed over a pan of
hot (not boiling) water.

Gently fold in the flour, cocoa powder and ground nuts. Put into
the prepared tin and bake for 20-25 minutes. Cool on a wire rack.

Set aside a quarter of the cream and a few strawberries. Gently
combine the remaining berries with the rest of the cream. Cut the
cake widthways into three equal pieces and sandwich together
with the filling. Spread the rest of the cream over the top and
sides of the cake. Sprinkle the sides of the cake with the toasted
nuts and decorate the top with the remaining sliced strawberries.

This is a great way of making a few strawberries go a long way.

Angel cake

75g/3 ounces plain (all-purpose) flour
50g/2 ounces cornflour (cornstarch)
115g/4 ounces icing (confectioner's) sugar
1 teaspoon cream of tartar
¼ teaspoon vanilla extract
10 egg whites
175g/6 ounces caster (superfine) sugar

Preheat the oven to 190°C/375°F/gas mark 5.

Sift the flour, cornflour and icing sugar twice into a mixing bowl.
Whisk together the cream of tartar, vanilla and egg whites in a
large grease-free bowl until the whites form soft peaks. Whisk in
the caster sugar until the mixture is stiff. Gently fold in the flour
mixture, a little at a time, until incorporated.

Spoon into an ungreased 25cm/10-inch tube or ring tin (pan).
Bake in the centre of the oven for about 45 minutes until the
cake springs back when lightly pressed with your fingertip.
Remove from the oven and invert the tin on a wire rack. Leave in
the inverted tin until cold.

Carefully release the cake from the tin and turn out onto a serving
plate. Serve alone or with whipped cream or ice cream and
summer berries.

*A wonderfully light, delicate cake made without fat. It's particularly delicious
with strawberries and cream. It's essential to use a tube or ring tin; an ordinary
cake tin will result in the outside drying out before the middle is cooked.*

Raspberry fool

450g/1 pound strawberries, sliced
225g/8 ounces raspberries
3 tablespoons icing (confectioner's) sugar, sifted
300ml/1¼ cups double (heavy) cream

Divide the strawberries among six ramekin dishes.

Sieve the raspberries (to remove the seeds) and stir in the icing
sugar. Whisk the cream until thick and stir in the raspberry mixture.

Spoon over the strawberries and chill for at least 30 minutes
before serving.

Sweet, juicy raspberries epitomize the taste of summer.
You can also use thawed frozen raspberries if you wish.

Punchstown chocolate

(Bradford Family Recipe)

4 eggs, separated
50g/2 ounces sugar
175g/6 ounces plain (dark) chocolate
½ teaspoon ground cinnamon
Squeeze of lemon juice
125ml/generous ½ cup sherry or fruit juice

Whisk the egg yolks and sugar in a bowl until thick and light.

Melt the chocolate in a heatproof bowl over a pan of simmering (not boiling) water or in a microwave oven. Allow to cool slightly.

Add the melted chocolate to the egg-yolk mixture, beating well. Stir in the cinnamon, lemon juice, sherry or juice.

Whisk the egg whites until stiff and gently fold into the mixture, a little at time. Pour into serving glasses or 1 large serving dish and chill for 6-8 hours before serving with whipped cream.

Chocolate mousse with a difference, but what a one! It could be described as a thoroughly modern recipe developed well before its time.

Brandy spiced peaches

300ml/1¼ cups water
225g/8 ounces caster (superfine) sugar
A little freshly grated nutmeg
1 cinnamon stick
10 peaches, skinned
4 tablespoons brandy

Put the water, sugar, nutmeg and cinnamon stick into a pan over a low heat until the sugar has completely dissolved. Bring to the boil and boil quickly for one minute, then remove the pan from the heat.

Cut each peach in half and remove the stone. Put the peach halves in the syrup and place over a low heat. Cook gently for 3-4 minutes. Leave the fruit in the syrup to cool, then stir in the brandy and chill for at least 4 hours before serving with whipped cream or vanilla ice cream.

The alcohol and sugar act as a preservative so the fruit will keep for months in a cool, dark place.

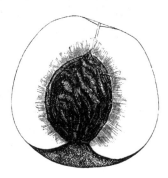

Raspberry ripple ice cream

50g/2 ounces plain (all-purpose) flour
4 egg yolks
75g/3 ounces caster (superfine) sugar
2 teaspoons vanilla extract
600ml/2½ cups creamy milk
300ml/1¼ cups whipping cream
225g/8 ounces fresh raspberries
2 tablespoons icing (confectioner's) sugar

Combine the flour, egg yolks, sugar and vanilla and stir in enough milk to make a thin paste. Heat the remaining milk and gradually stir into the paste, making sure there are no lumps.

Pour into a pan and slowly bring to the boil, stirring all the time. Reduce the heat and cook gently for 3 minutes. Remove from the heat, cover with a piece of damp greaseproof (waxed) paper to prevent a skin forming and leave until cold.

Whisk the cream until thick, but not stiff, and fold into the cold custard. Transfer to a freezer-proof container and freeze for 3-4 hours, or until partly frozen.

Sieve the raspberries and stir in the icing sugar. Remove the ice cream from the freezer, beat it well and lightly swirl in the raspberry mixture to give a 'rippled' effect. Return to the freezer until solid. Transfer to the refrigerator 20-30 minutes before serving.

Fresh, homemade ice creams taste so much better than bought ones. Using fresh cream, fruit and other wholesome ingredients gives quite a different flavour and texture to that of commercial ice cream – and the added bonus is that ice cream made at home contains no emulsifiers, 'E-numbers' or artificial colouring or flavouring.

You don't need any special equipment, although if you do own an ice-cream maker the results will be even better. There are a few simple rules for successful ice-cream making – see below.

•*Switch the freezer to 'fast freeze' a few hours before you start; the faster the ice cream freezes, the better the texture.*

•*Always ensure that all utensils are scrupulously clean. Ice cream can provide an ideal breeding ground for undesirable bacteria.*

•*Once thawed, ice cream must never be re-frozen.*

•*Use a strong, plastic freezer box with a lid to freeze the mixture.*

•*Homemade ice cream is best eaten within two weeks because it doesn't contain the additives of the commercial product, so won't keep for the same length of time.*

Banana custard ice cream

1 x 400g/14-ounce can condensed milk
2 tablespoons custard powder
3 eggs, separated
4 bananas
Juice of 1 lemon

Make up the condensed milk to
900ml/1 quart with cold water.
Blend the custard powder with a little of
the milk to make a smooth paste.

Heat the remaining milk in a pan to boiling point and pour onto
the paste, mixing well. Return to the pan and bring to the boil
again, stirring all the time, and cook until the mixture thickens.
Remove from the heat and allow to cool slightly.

Beat the egg yolks and add the hot custard. Mash the bananas
with the lemon juice and beat into the custard. Leave until cold,
stirring now and again.

Pour into a freezer-proof container, cover and freeze until just
becoming firm. Turn the mixture into a bowl and beat well.

Whisk the egg whites until stiff and fold into the ice cream.
Spoon back into the container, cover and freeze until firm. Place
in the refrigerator about 30 minutes before serving.

Use ripe bananas for the best flavour. Peel the bananas just before using and
mix immediately with the lemon juice to prevent discolouration.

Iced tea punch

6 Earl Grey tea bags
3 tablespoons sugar
5cm/2-inch piece cinnamon stick
1.2 litres/5 cups boiling water
Juice of 2 oranges
Juice of 1 lemon

Put the tea bags, sugar and cinnamon stick into a large jug and pour on the boiling water.

Leave to infuse for 5-10 minutes, then strain and add the fruit juices. Serve chilled.

An ideal drink for children, teetotallers and drivers, although if you want to give it an alcoholic kick, add a slug of brandy or rum.

The original English punch was made of claret, brandy, lemon and orange juices, sugar and a little nutmeg and was introduced to England by merchants of the East India Company in the seventeenth century. The name 'punch' derived from the Hindu word panch, *meaning 'five' – a reference to its five ingredients (sugar, spirits, fruit juice, water and flavourings), and in India it had been enjoyed as a long, refreshing drink for over 2,000 years. In England, it was served from a large bowl with a piece of toasted bread or biscuits (cookies) floating on the top.*

WAKES AND FAIRS
THE WAKES HOLIDAY

Long ago in the north of England, the feast days of local saints used to be known as 'wakes' and in the West Country as 'revels'. The term 'wake' is the same as the one applied to funerals and refers to the custom of keeping vigil all night in the parish church on the eve of the saint's feast day, before mass was celebrated at dawn. In the Middle Ages, wakes were sober occasions, when parishioners fasted and did penance, but after the Reformation they became lively social events, with fairs, music and dancing. Many people attended the wakes with less devotion and reverence, and gradually, hawkers, pedlars and merchants set up their stalls in churchyards.

The more important the saint whose feast was being celebrated, the bigger the turnout – and thus was created the fair. The fairs were also an opportunity to raise funds for the local church, because all the proceeds were given to the parish priest.

In Lancashire, such fairs continued to be known as wakes, and later on came to mean an annual holiday when the cotton mills closed. Summer wakes were the most popular and these eventually turned into an annual holiday for the whole town. 'Wakes weeks' are now only a distant memory for a very few, but in some counties today, the annual village feast day is still celebrated with sports, feasting and a church parade.

Great preparations were made for the wakes, and many regions made their own special foods for the celebration. Sweet foods, always a luxury in the past, were reserved as a treat for special occasions, with cakes, buns and biscuits (cookies) being the most popular. Specially made 'wakes cakes' were baked in vast numbers to be sold very cheaply or given away. Early types of these cakes were nothing more than plain bread dough enriched with eggs, fat, dried fruits and spices, but as time passed and ingredients such as sugar and spices became cheaper, wakes cakes became correspondingly richer.

The traditional wakes holiday was often accompanied by the arrival of a travelling fairground. The advent of the railways in the nineteenth century enabled many mill workers to travel to the seaside; Blackpool was particularly popular. Entire streets of people spent an enjoyable carefree week by the sea in stark contrast to the grimy industrial cotton towns they lived in. The wakes festivities and fairs continued in Blackpool, with the building of the Big Wheel and the Pleasure Beach.

Towns held their wakes-weeks holiday at different times. Although the cotton industry is no more, the wakes weeks are still enjoyed in Lancashire's towns.

The majority of Britain's fairs can trace their origins back to charters and privileges granted in the Middle Ages. In the thirteenth century, the granting of a royal charter for fairs was common, with the Crown receiving revenue in return for the control of the fair to stay with a particular town, abbey or village.

A charter granted in 1284 by Edward I authorized Nottingham to hold a fair on the eve of the Feast of St Edmund and for 12 days following. Another fair mentioned was the St Matthew's Fair, held on September 21, which is said to date back to Anglo-Saxon times. Some charters were granted to fairs that already existed, such as Nottingham Goose Fair, which was also granted a charter by Edward I in 1284.

Hiring fairs, or 'mop fairs', were created in the fourteenth century with the passing of the Statute of Labourers in 1351 by Edward III. These continued in their original purpose of hiring servants and labourers until the end of the nineteenth century, when the original intention of the event was superseded by the amusements. Generations of children have enjoyed sweet, sugary fairground delicacies such as glistening toffee (caramel) apples, airy clouds of candy floss (cotton candy) and garishly coloured rock (stick candy), and tried to dislodge a hairy brown coconut at the coconut shy. Coconuts were unknown in England until the eighteenth century, but it wasn't until the nineteenth century that they began to be imported and became a fashionable novelty. Desiccated (shredded) coconut became available in the late nineteenth century and was an instant hit as a popular baking ingredient.

Toffee apples were originally a medieval luxury for the wealthy nobility of England. They were sold at the numerous fairs held to celebrate religious feasts and were made by coating apples with a mixture of boiling honey and beeswax. Toffee apples have remained a fairground treat, although nowadays affordable by everyone. The contrast of crisp, fresh apple flesh with the sweet, brittle toffee is delightful.

Rock was invented in the nineteenth century, when it was known as rock candy. A confection of boiled sugar flavoured with peppermint, it is most familiar as a lurid pink stick with tiny red lettering running right the way through it. Tastes in rock have changed over the years, and although sticks of rock are still popular, nowadays they come in all sorts of colours and flavours. There's also a huge selection of shapes to choose from: baskets of 'fruit', cardboard plates of 'bacon and eggs', 'false teeth' and even realistic looking 'kippers' are all made entirely of rock and destined to be bought as gifts for friends.

Candy floss, or cotton candy, a light, airy confection of spun sugar, was first made around 1900 as a fairground treat. Children today still love to watch, fascinated as the sugar and pink colouring are sprinkled into a stainless-steel drum, a wooden stick is placed in the centre and the attendant switches on the machine. The drum rapidly spins the sugar around the stick to produce the familiar puffy pink cloud and its sweet, sticky scent of hot sugar.

Fairings were biscuits (cookies) sold at fairs in the Middle Ages. They usually contained ginger and other spices and were sold as round or square, simple biscuits or baked in elaborate wooden moulds, then gilded and studded with cloves. Moulded fairings took the form of hearts, flowers, birds and human figures. Ordinary people eagerly looked forward to these fairground delicacies – a wonderful treat in their austere everyday diet. Fairings were also bought to take back as presents for those unable to attend the fair.

Cherry fairs, held to celebrate a successful harvest, were one of the most popular festivals in cherry-growing areas, particularly in Kent, which is still famous for the excellent cherries that have flourished in the region's fertile soil since Roman times. By the sixteenthh century, Kent had become the chief cherry-growing area in England.

People sang and danced in the orchards and took part in cherry-eating contests, while cherry sellers sold the luscious scarlet fruits to visitors. English medieval monks cultivated cherry trees in monastery gardens, and judging from their inclusion in the paintings of the period, it's clear that they were highly prized. They were also popular in London's street markets of the past, when the fruit was brought to London on carts from Kent. The cherry sellers cried their wares in the streets: 'Cherries-O! Cherries ripe, all ripe, round and sound ripe cherries, fine duke cherries ... only five-pence a pound! Cherries ripe, cherries ripe, all ripe!'

In Stuart times, Rotherhithe was famous for its Cherry Gardens. The gardens were a popular recreational area, and Londoners often spent a pleasant Saturday afternoon relaxing there. Samuel Pepys mentions visiting the area in his famous diary to buy cherries for his wife.

The great English horse fairs in England were an annual event for centuries and were an opportunity for travelling Romany people to meet up with family and friends. Only two horse fairs have survived: at Appleby, in Cumbria, and Stow–on-the-Wold, in Gloucestershire. Appleby horse fair was first held in 1685 and is the best known of the Romany horse fairs, where gypsy families still meet up to celebrate their history, music and folklore – and of course, to do business.

Lancashire wakes cakes

225g/8 ounces plain (all-purpose) flour
Pinch salt
175g/1¾ sticks butter
25g/1 ounce caster (superfine) sugar, plus extra for sprinkling
Milk to mix (if needed)
75g/3 ounces dried fruit
1 egg, beaten

Preheat the oven to 180°C/350°F/gas mark 4. Butter a large baking tray.

Sift the flour and salt into a mixing bowl and rub in the butter until the mixture resembles breadcrumbs. Stir in the sugar and dried fruit. Add the beaten egg and mix to a soft dough, adding a little milk if necessary.

Knead lightly and roll out to 5mm/¼-inch thickness. Use a saucer to cut into rounds and place these on the buttered baking tray. Bake for about 15 minutes until golden. Remove from the oven and sprinkle with caster sugar.

These delicious, buttery cakes have a melt-in-the-mouth texture and are best eaten as fresh as possible. Any dried fruit can be used – currants, sultanas (white raisins), chopped dates, etc.

Lancashire nuts

(Bradford Family Recipe)

225g/2¼ sticks butter
225g/8 ounces sugar
1 egg
115g/4 ounces cornflour (cornstarch)
225g/8 ounces plain (all-purpose) flour
½ teaspoon baking powder

Preheat the oven to 200°C/400°F/gas mark 6. Grease a large
baking tray.

Cream the butter and sugar until light. Beat in the egg until
well blended. Sift in the cornflour, flour and baking powder and
mix to a soft dough.

Shape into small balls and place well apart on the baking tray.
Flatten slightly and bake for about 15-20 minutes until golden.

*Why Lancashire nuts? There must be a reason, but nobody seems to know
or even recall them properly, as the mists of time have surely done their work.
However, they're rather unusual, little savoury biscuits (cookies) – so just
try them. RB*

Ginger fairings

50g/½ stick butter
115g/4 ounces dark muscovado (soft dark brown) sugar
2 tablespoons black treacle (molasses)
175g/6 ounces plain (all-purpose) flour
Pinch of salt
2 teaspoons ground ginger
¼ teaspoon ground mixed spice
¼ teaspoon ground cinnamon

Preheat the oven to 160°C/325°F/gas mark 3. Grease 2 large baking trays.

Cream the butter and dark muscovado sugar together until soft and creamy. Stir in the treacle, mixing well, and then sift in the flour, salt and spices.

Work the mixture to a stiff dough. Roll out on a lightly floured surface and cut into 5cm/2-inch rounds with a biscuit (cookie) cutter. Place the rounds on the baking trays and bake for 15 minutes. Remove from the oven and cool on a wire rack.

Sticky black, viscous treacle has a strong taste and is used to add flavour, colour and moisture to gingerbreads and biscuits (cookies).

Coconut macaroons

2 egg whites
2 teaspoons cornflour (cornstarch)
115g/4 ounces caster (superfine) sugar
115g/4 ounces shredded coconut

Preheat the oven to 180°C/350°F/gas mark 4. Line one or two baking trays with rice paper or non-stick baking paper.

Place the egg whites in a bowl and whisk until frothy, but not stiff. Stir in the cornflour and sugar, followed by the coconut. Drop in heaps onto the lined trays. Bake for about 20 minutes until firm and golden brown. Leave to cool. When cold, store in an airtight tin.

Coconut macaroons are a very English type of cake and a favourite item in teashops and cafés around the country. Try serving them with strawberries and cream or with any of the ice creams here. In the seventeenth century, macaroons were traditionally made with almonds, and they were served accompanied by sherry or wine.

Gypsy tart

115g/4 ounces plain (all-purpose) flour
Pinch of salt
50g/½ stick butter, cut into cubes
Water to mix
1 x 400g/14-ounce can evaporated milk, chilled
275g/9½ ounces unrefined dark muscovado (soft dark brown) sugar

Preheat the oven to 200°C/400°F/gas mark 6. Grease a 20cm/
8-inch flan tin or pie dish.

Sift the flour into a mixing bowl and stir in the salt. Rub in the
butter with your fingers, until the mixture looks like breadcrumbs.
Slowly add just enough water to mix to a soft, smooth dough.

Sprinkle the work surface with flour and roll out the pastry evenly
until it is big enough to line the flan tin. Carefully lift the pastry
onto the rolling pin and lay this over the tin. Ease the pastry into
the dish, pressing it gently against the sides and base. Cover the
base with a sheet of greaseproof (waxed) paper and weigh this
down with some baking beans, uncooked pasta or rice – this
stops the pastry rising while it is baking. Bake for 15-20 minutes,
then remove the beans and paper and leave to cool.

Pour the chilled evaporated milk and muscovado sugar into a
bowl. Using an electric mixer, whisk together until light, creamy
and coffee-coloured; this will take 12-15 minutes. Pour the
mixture into the cool pastry case and bake for 20 minutes.

Remove from the oven and leave to cool. As it cools, the filling
sets and will be ready to eat when it is just warm.

*A much-loved old favourite. Dark muscovado sugar gives the creamy filling a
delectable rich toffee flavour. It's important to use unrefined muscovado sugar
as the natural molasses in the crystals binds and holds the mixture together.*

Toffee (caramel) apples

8 eating (dessert) apples
450g/1 pound sugar
115g/1 stick butter
2 tablespoons water

Wipe the apples well to remove any waxy coating, otherwise
the toffee won't stick. Remove the stalks and put a wooden stick
in each stalk end.

Heat the sugar, butter and water in a pan over a low heat until
dissolved. Bring to the boil and cook until a little of the mixture
forms a soft crack (140°C/280°F on a sugar/candy thermometer)
when dropped into cold water. Remove from the heat.

Dip the apples into the toffee, swirling them around until
well-coated, then dip them into a bowl of iced water. Place on
non-stick baking paper. Eat within a couple of hours; the apples
become sticky if left longer.

*Toffee apples are easy to make at home – although they are best eaten on the
day they're made.*

Uncooked coconut ice

6 tablespoons sweetened condensed milk
250-300g/9-10 ounces golden icing (confectioner's) sugar, sifted
175g/6 ounces desiccated coconut
Pink food colouring (optional)

Mix the condensed milk and golden icing sugar in a large bowl, then stir in the coconut; the mixture will be stiff.

Divide the mixture in two and colour one half with a few drops of food colouring if you wish. Shape the mixture into two rectangles and press firmly together.

Dust a tin (pan) or board with icing sugar and leave the coconut ice on this until firm. Cut into bars or squares to serve.

Because no cooking is involved, this is ideal for younger children to make.
The mixture is very stiff, though, so they may need help with the mixing.

Nougat

Rice paper for lining loaf tin
125ml/½ cup honey
115g/4 ounces icing (confectioner's) sugar, plus extra for dredging
2 egg whites
225g/8 ounces blanched almonds, chopped

Line a loaf tin (pan) with rice paper; this is easier if you dampen the tin slightly first.

Place the honey, sugar and egg whites into a heavy saucepan and heat gently, stirring constantly to the firm-ball stage (120°C/250°F on a sugar/candy thermometer), when the mixture will be thick and white. Remove from the heat and stir in the almonds.

Turn out onto a surface dredged with icing sugar and form into a ball. Press into the prepared tin, cover with rice paper, then with a piece of baking parchment. Place a heavy weight on top and leave overnight.

Cut into slices and wrap in greaseproof (waxed) paper.

Wrapped nougat will keep for about two weeks in an airtight tin.

Peanut brittle

225g/8 ounces sugar
2 tablespoons water
2 tablespoons unsalted roasted peanuts
15g/½ ounce butter
Few drops vanilla extract
¼ teaspoon bicarbonate of soda (baking soda)

Heat the sugar and water in a heavy pan over a low heat, without stirring, until dissolved (if the mixture is stirred the sugar will crystallize). Increase the heat and boil quickly, stirring, for about 5 minutes until syrupy. Remove from the heat.

Add the peanuts, butter and vanilla. Stir quickly and stir in the bicarbonate of soda (baking soda). Pour into a buttered tin and leave to set. Break into pieces when cold.

Sweet, buttery nut brittle is an old-fashioned sweet that's easy to make. You can substitute walnuts or almonds for the peanuts if you prefer.

Creamy fudge

450g/1 pound sugar
1 x 400g/14-ounce (approx.) can sweetened condensed milk
175g/1½ sticks butter
1 teaspoon vanilla extract

Grease a Swiss roll tin (pan) with butter.

Put the sugar, condensed milk and butter in a large, heavy
saucepan and place over a low heat, stirring with a wooden spoon
until the sugar has completely dissolved. Turn up the heat and
bring to the boil. Boil steadily for 10 minutes, stirring all the time.

Take the pan off the heat and stir in the vanilla extract. Return to
the heat and bring back to the boil. Boil the mixture for 2-3
minutes, or until it begins to look dry against the sides of the pan.

Take off the heat and beat the mixture with a wooden spoon
until it becomes 'grainy' and feels gritty. Pour quickly into the
buttered tin and leave to set. Cut into squares when cold.

*The crumblier texture and rich flavour of homemade fudge is so much nicer
than the commercially made version.*

Cumberland buttermilk cake

450g/1 pound plain (all-purpose) flour
75g/¾ stick butter
115g/4 ounces sugar
350g/12 ounces mixed dried fruit
2 tablespoons orange marmalade
½ teaspoon ground cinnamon (optional)
150ml/⅝ cup buttermilk or sour milk
1 teaspoon bicarbonate of soda (baking soda)

Preheat the oven to 160°C/325°F/gas mark 3. Grease a 20cm/
8-inch round cake tin (pan).

Sift the flour into a large mixing bowl and rub in the butter until
the mixture resembles breadcrumbs. Stir in the sugar, dried fruit,
marmalade and cinnamon, if using.

Heat the buttermilk until warm and stir in the soda. Add to the
cake mixture, stirring to form a soft dough. Put into the cake tin
and cook for 1 hour. Reduce the heat to 150°C/300°F/gas mark 2
and continue baking for another 35-45 minutes, or until cooked
through. Remove from the oven and leave to cool in the tin for 10
minutes, then turn out onto a wire rack and leave to become cold.

Cakes and sweetmeats unique to each region were sold at summer fairs, and
while some of these regional delicacies have died out, others have become
universal favourites. Buttermilk, left in the churn after butter-making, was
considered a great delicacy as far back as Tudor era. It has a delicate but
distinctive flavour and its acidity makes wonderfully light scones and cakes.

Cherries jubilee

450g/1 pound cherries, stones removed
110ml/½ cup water
50g/2 ounces sugar
1 cinnamon stick
Grated zest and juice of 1 small orange
1 teaspoon cornflour (cornstarch)
1 tablespoon kirsch or cherry
brandy (optional)

Put the cherries and water in a pan
and bring to the boil. Boil for 8 minutes
then strain, reserving the juices.

Set the cherries aside and return the juices to the pan with the
remaining ingredients except the kirsch. Bring to the boil and boil
rapidly until reduced to a thick syrup. Remove the cinnamon stick
and stir in the kirsch if using.

Serve warm with low-fat yogurt or crème fraiche.

Wash cherries quickly under cold running water – never soak them.
Colour is usually a good indicator of flavour; generally, the darker the fruit,
the sweeter it is.

Cherry ripe flan

225g/8 ounces shortcrust (medium-flake) pastry
450g/1 pound cherries, stones removed
3 eggs
50g/2 ounces sugar
300ml/1¼ cups whipping cream
1 teaspoon almond extract

Preheat the oven to 200°C/400°F/gas mark 6. Grease a 23cm/
9-inch loose-based fluted flan tin (pan) or pie dish.

Roll out the pastry on a floured surface and line the tin. Bake blind
for 10-15 minutes. Reduce the oven temperature to 180°C/350°F/
gas mark 4.

Arrange the cherries in the flan tin. Beat the eggs with the sugar,
cream and almond extract until blended. Slowly pour over the
cherries carefully, taking care not to dislodge them. Bake for
about 30 minutes, or until the custard is set.

Cool in the tin on a wire rack, then remove the sides of the tin to
finish cooling. Serve warm or cold.

Queen Victoria had a sweet tooth, and sweets and puddings were among her
favourite dishes. She was especially fond of cherries and loved to eat them
with plenty of cream.

Fresh cherry ice cream

115g/4 ounces caster (superfine) sugar
150ml/⅝ cup water
Juice of half a small lemon
250g/9 ounces ripe cherries, stones removed
500g/1 pound mascarpone cheese
1 tablespoon kirsch

Heat the sugar, water and lemon juice in a pan over a low heat until the sugar has dissolved completely. Bring to the boil and boil for 3 minutes. Reduce the heat, add the cherries and simmer gently for about 10 minutes, or until the cherries are soft. Remove from the heat and leave to stand until completely cold.

Beat the mascarpone in a bowl to soften. Beat in the syrup, juice from the cherries and the kirsch until combined. Gently fold in the cherries, swirling them through the mixture. Spoon into a freezer-proof container, cover and freeze until required.

Transfer the ice cream to the refrigerator about 25 minutes before serving, to allow it to soften slightly.

Mascarpone gives this ice cream a delicious creamy texture and flavour. Stone the cherries over a bowl to catch the juices.

Autumn

HARVEST

Since antiquity, the gathering in of the harvest from fields and orchards has been an occasion for celebration and feasting. The Anglo-Saxons called the first day of harvesting 'lammas,' a word derived from the Saxon *llafmaesse,* or 'loaf mass', which was a special loaf made from the first of the newly harvested grain. The words 'lord' and 'lady' are derived from the Anglo-Saxon *hlaford* and *hlaedige,* meaning 'loaf ward' or 'master' and 'loaf kneader' or 'wife', respectively.

In the Highlands of Scotland, the new grain was made into a bannock (a round, flat loaf cooked on a griddle) known as *moilean Moire* 'the fatling of Mary', because Lammas coincided with the Feast of St Mary the Great). This bannock was toasted over a fire of rowan or other sacred wood and it was customary for the husband to break the loaf into small pieces for his wife and children, sized according to their age. The family wore their best clothes and sang a hymn to Mary as they walked round the fire.

In Orkney it was a Lammas custom to make a bannock of flour, melted butter and fruit, which was given as a reward to the man who carried the last load of sheaves into the stack-yard.

In Ireland it was known as *La-ith-mas* (the day of the obligation of grain), which became Lammas and was dedicated to the sacrifice of the fruits of the soil.

All over the UK, the last sheaf of grain, or 'corn' as grain is often known here, to be cut was treated with great reverence and was intricately plaited into a 'corn dolly', which was believed to contain the harvest spirit. The corn dolly was variously known as a corn baby, harvest queen or maiden and was sometimes dressed in a white dress and decorated with ribbons. It was borne aloft at the head of a procession and carried with great ceremony to the barn where the harvest supper was held. In Scotland, the corn dolly was dressed as an old woman with a cap, dress, shawl and apron and given pride of place at the harvest supper. Corn dollies were frequently saved until the next harvest, when they would be burned with much ceremony, or saved to be planted the following spring to ensure another good harvest.

With the advent of Christianity, a cross made from corn or wheat sheaves replaced the pagan corn dolly. In medieval Yorkshire, the cross was placed over the door of York Minster, and the inside of the church was decorated with wheat and specially baked loaves dedicated to God, which were blessed by the priest.

Bread had an important role at this time of year, and it was generally believed that to eat newly baked bread made from the first of the new grain would ensure a full larder for the coming year. Special cakes were also made for harvest time. The earliest were made from leftover bread dough enriched with fat and eggs and sprinkled with dried fruits and spices. As sugar, dried fruits and spices became cheaper and more easily available, each county and region developed their own recipes for breads and rich, fruited cakes, such as Suffolk fourses, which were carried to the labourers in the fields, where they were accompanied by beer, cider or lemonade. Suffolk fourses may have been named from the practice of cutting the round or square cakes into four, or possibly because it was customary to eat them at the four o'clock break.

The harvest feast originated in feudal England, when the lord of the manor provided special food and drink for the workers, who laboured from dawn to dusk in the fields. As time passed, it was farmers and their wives who became responsible for feeding the large numbers of casual workers and their families who were taken on at harvest time.

Harvesting was gruelling work, and men, women and children toiled in the fields from dawn till dusk. Church bells were rung in some counties at 5am – the start of each harvesting day – and again at 7pm to mark the end of the day's work. Children were a vital part of the workforce and were given a long holiday from school from July to September.

The harvest supper was a celebratory meal for the farm hands, casual workers and their families. In Northumberland, the meal was called the 'mell supper' (*mell* meaning 'meal' or 'grain'); in East Anglia it was known as the 'horkey', and in parts of Yorkshire as the 'innings goose', as goose was the main dish.

Vast quantities of food and drink were provided to satisfy large appetites sharpened from the fresh air. The huge array of food included boiled hams, roast meats, stews and pies (the farmers' wives made good use of the rabbits and hares caught in the fields during reaping), and cheeses made from early summer milk, which would have matured nicely in time for the feast. Sweet dishes included cakes, tarts and pies, the latter often made using seasonal fruits such as blackberries and apples. Copious quantities of ale and cider were provided, and everyone took part in games, singing and dancing.

The food served at the meal depended on what was grown locally. Lardy cakes were popular in pig-rearing areas such as Wiltshire and Hampshire. Splendidly rich and sticky, lardy cake was made by spreading a rectangle of bread dough with dried fruits, (chopped apples were often added in orchard-growing areas), sugar, spices and lard, folding and rolling it several times, rather like puff pastry, before baking until crisp and golden.

A Welsh relative of lardy cake was *bara brith,* or 'speckled bread'. This delicious fruit tea-bread is still popular today and is sold all over Wales, although nowadays it is usually made without yeast. In Carmarthenshire, the harvest supper included a dish called *whipod* made with rice, white bread, raisins, currants and treacle. After the meal, there was dancing to fiddle music and an abundant supply of beer and tobacco.

Oats were also part of the staple diet of the Welsh, and were a basic ingredient of many dishes such as *sucan blawd* (oatmeal husks soaked in water until sour, then strained and boiled to a pale-brown, gelatinous mass) which was usually eaten with fresh milk.

Dough cakes speckled with fruit were made in the south and southwestern regions of England. They were similar to lardy cakes, the difference being that the ingredients were kneaded into the dough. Those who were too poor to own an oven took their dried fruit, lard, spices and sugar to the local baker, who added some dough and returned a beautifully cooked cake.

Lincolnshire plum bread, a sweet, spiced, fruited loaf, has a long history. Despite the name, there are no plums in the recipe. 'Plum' was used in the past as a generic term (much like corn today) and refers to the dried fruits, namely currants, raisins and sultanas (white raisins). The rich, moist loaf is more like a fruit cake than bread and was often eaten with cheese.

Harvest Betsy cake was an early type of cake made with barley flour, wheat flour and a little dried fruit. Vinegar cake was an economical cake that was very popular with those who couldn't afford eggs; the vinegar reacted with the milk and soda to produce a light texture.

In Yorkshire, shrewd farmers made sure that caraway seeds were incorporated into loaves and cakes for the harvest supper, as the aromatic seeds were reputed to impart strength and also discourage the eater from stealing!

Potatoes were the main crop in Lancashire, and a successful potato harvest was celebrated with a 'shut in' in the barn. Potatoes appeared in various guises in both savoury and sweet dishes: Lancashire hotpot was served piping hot; potato cakes, cooked on a griddle were very popular, while another favourite, farmhouse pudding, was a sweet, boiled pudding made with mashed potatoes, carrots, dried fruits and spices. Other tasty potato dishes were also enjoyed accompanied by the singing of traditional songs.

By the end of the nineteenth century, harvest feasts had developed into church suppers. The first 'Harvest Thanksgiving' in 1843 was the idea of a Cornish vicar, the Reverend Hawker, who, during a service of thanksgiving, invited his parishioners to take communion made from the 'bread of the new corn'. After the service he blessed the crops, and everyone enjoyed a communal meal in the church hall, after which some of the produce was given to the poor; thus the modern 'harvest festival' was created, which still takes place in most English towns and villages today. Churches are still beautifully decorated with seasonal fruits and vegetables as well as decorative sheaves of corn and wheat, and everyone brings a gift of food which is given by the church to the poor and needy of the parish.

Harvest beef

900g/2 pounds stewing steak, cubed
2 onions, sliced
Pinch of ground cloves
Pinch of ground mace
5 black peppercorns
½ teaspoon salt
75ml/generous ¼ cup cider vinegar
50g/2 ounces dark muscovado (soft dark brown) sugar
600ml/2½ cups dark beer
2 sprigs thyme
2 bay leaves

Put the meat and onions into a large bowl. Combine the spices and salt with the cider vinegar and sugar and pour over the beef. Cover and leave to stand overnight, turning the meat from time to time.

Next day, tip the contents of the bowl into a large pan and pour in the beer. Add the herbs. Bring to the boil, then reduce the heat and simmer for about 2 hours, or until the meat is tender.

This rich, tasty stew was a favourite with haymakers after a long day in the fields.

Cumberland tatie pot

1kg/2¼ pounds stewing steak or lamb, cut into pieces
2 large onions, sliced
5 carrots, sliced
2 bay leaves
2 sprigs fresh thyme
350g/12 ounces black pudding (blood sausage), sliced
Salt and pepper
600ml/2½ cups full-flavoured ale
3-4 large potatoes, sliced

Preheat the oven to 150°C/300°F/gas mark 2.

Layer the meat, vegetables (except the potatoes) and black pudding in a deep, ovenproof baking dish or roasting tin (pan), seasoning each layer with salt and pepper.

Cover with a layer of potatoes. Pour in the beer to come almost to the top – the exact amount will depend on the size and depth of your dish or tin. Cover and cook for about 2-2½ hours, or until the meat is tender – the exact time will depend on the size of the dish.

Remove the lid and increase the oven temperature to 180°C/350°F/gas mark 4 and continue cooking for 35-45 minutes, or until the potatoes are browned.

This famous speciality used to be sold in large earthenware jars in public houses in Cumbria and was an essential dish at local hunt meetings and shepherds' meets. Tatie pot suppers were also popular local events in the area. This traditional regional recipe is made heartier and richer with the addition of full-flavoured ale.

Baked spiced ham

1 x 2kg/4½-pound boned and rolled gammon (ham) joint
2 onions, quartered
4 peppercorns
2 carrots
Parsley stalks
2 bay leaves
Few sprigs of fresh thyme
2 teaspoons ground allspice
1 teaspoon ground cloves
1 teaspoon ground cinnamon
1 teaspoon ground bay leaves
115g/4 ounces demerara (light brown cane) sugar
100ml/½ cup dry cider (applejack) or beer

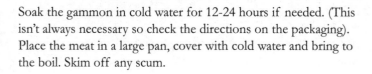

Soak the gammon in cold water for 12-24 hours if needed. (This isn't always necessary so check the directions on the packaging). Place the meat in a large pan, cover with cold water and bring to the boil. Skim off any scum.

Add the onions, cloves, parsley, bay leaves and thyme. Cover and slowly simmer for 1½ hours.

Preheat the oven to 200°C/400°F/gas mark 6. Place the gammon in a roasting tin (pan) and remove the skin, leaving the fat intact. Pour in the cider or beer. Mix the sugar with the spices and rub all over the ham. Bake for 30 minutes, basting frequently with the cider or beer.

When the fat is golden and crisp, transfer to a warm plate and leave until cold.

A moist, succulent ham makes a wonderful centrepiece for a family meal.

Game pie

2 tablespoons oil
1 wood pigeon, jointed
1 grouse, jointed
Meat from half a hare, cut into pieces
225g/8 ounces venison, cut into pieces
Salt and pepper
50g/½ stick butter
115g/4 ounces large field mushrooms, chopped
1 onion, finely chopped
2 bay leaves
1 sprig fresh sage
115g/4 ounces bacon, diced
300ml/1¼ cups red wine
225-350g/8-12 ounces puff pastry, depending on the size of dish
1 egg, beaten to glaze

Preheat the oven to 170°C/350°F/gas mark 3.

Heat the oil in a frying pan and brown the game-bird joints on all
sides. Place the joints in a deep casserole or ovenproof dish. Brown
the hare and venison in the same oil and add to the casserole dish.
Season to taste with salt and pepper.

Heat the butter in the same frying pan and cook the mushrooms
and onion until for a few minutes until softened. Add the herbs
and wine to the pan and bring to the boil. Pour over the meats in
the casserole; if it doesn't cover the meat, add more wine or water.
Cover and cook for about 1½ hours, until the birds are tender.

Remove the birds from the casserole, and when cool enough to
handle, strip the meat from the bones and return the meat to the
casserole. Leave to stand to become cold. Skim off any fat.

Preheat the oven to 220°C/425°F/gas mark 7.

Roll out the pastry dough and place on top of the dish. Use any spare pastry to make pastry leaves, etc., to decorate the pie. Brush with beaten egg and bake for 20 minutes, then reduce the oven temperature to 200°C/400°F/gas mark 6 and cook for another 20 minutes, or until the pastry is golden and the filling is piping hot. Serve hot with vegetables.

This is a good way of using older, tougher game meat. You can use a brace of pheasant or grouse instead of the pigeon and grouse if you prefer. Wood pigeon live on corn and other cereals and are at their best in the autumn. Red grouse, native to Scottish and north Yorkshire moors, feed on heather, berries and herbs which imbue their flesh with a unique flavour. They are in season from August 13 (known as The Glorious 12th – the start of the shooting season) until December 10.

Cornish caudle pie

25g/¼ stick butter
1 tablespoon oil
1 onion, peeled and finely chopped
2 boneless, skinless chicken breasts
2 tablespoons chopped fresh parsley
Salt and pepper
A little grated nutmeg
150ml/⅝ cup milk
225g/8 ounces puff pastry
150ml/⅝ cup single (light) cream
2 eggs, beaten

Preheat the oven to 180°C/350°F/gas mark 4.

Heat the butter and oil in a frying pan and cook the onion until soft but not brown. Place in a 1.2 litre/generous quart pie dish. Add the chicken to the pan and cook for a few minutes until browned all over. Arrange on top of the onion in the dish.

Add the parsley, salt and pepper, nutmeg and milk to the pan and bring to the boil. Simmer for 2 minutes, then pour over the chicken. Cover the dish and cook in the oven for about 30 minutes, or until the chicken is tender. Remove from the oven and leave to cool.

Increase the oven temperature to 220°C/425°F/gas mark 7. Roll out the pastry dough about 2.5cm/1 inch larger all round than the pie dish. Cut off a strip from all round the edge of the pastry and place the strip on the rim of the pie dish. Moisten with a little water and place the pastry lid on top. Press to seal the edges and make a small hole in the centre of the pastry lid.

Beat the eggs and cream together and use a little of the mixture to brush the top of the pie. Bake for 15-20 minutes until golden, then reduce the oven temperature to 180°C/350°F/gas mark 4. Pour the egg and cream mixture through the hole in the pastry lid and shake the dish to distribute the mixture evenly. Return to the oven for 15 minutes.

Remove from the oven and leave to stand in a warm place for 10 minutes before serving.

This is a modern version of a medieval recipe, when a mixture of egg yolks, cream, white wine and spices were poured into the filling towards the end of cooking time.

Beef and cheese pie

2 tablespoons oil
1 large onion, chopped
2 cloves garlic, finely chopped
225g/8 ounces lean minced beef
1 tablespoon tomato purée
½ teaspoon ground mace
¼ teaspoon grated nutmeg
75g/3 ounces Cheddar cheese, grated

<u>For the dough case</u>
225g/8 ounces strong (bread) flour
1 teaspoon bicarbonate of soda (baking soda)
1 teaspoon cream of tartar
1 teaspoon salt
150ml/⅝ cup milk

Preheat the oven to 200°C/400°F/gas mark 6. Lightly grease a deep 23cm/9-inch flan or pie dish.

Heat the oil and cook the onion gently until soft but not brown. Add the garlic, increase the heat and add the minced beef. Stir well and add the spices and tomato purée. Season to taste with salt and pepper and leave to cool.

Sift the dry ingredients into a mixing bowl and stir in the milk to form a soft dough. Knead lightly on a floured surface and roll out to a 26-30cm/10-12-inch circle. Ease the dough into the flan dish, pressing well against the base and sides. Spoon in the meat mixture, spreading it evenly and cover with the cheese. Bake for about 30 minutes, or until the bread case is cooked through.

This is slightly unusual because the case for the meat and cheese filling is made from bread dough.

Toad in the hole

450g/1 pound Porters handmade or good-quality pork sausages
1 tablespoon oil
225g/8 ounces plain (all-purpose) flour
Pinch of salt
2 eggs
600ml/2½ cups milk
1 tablespoon chopped fresh herbs (optional)

Preheat the oven to 220°C/425°F/gas mark 7.

Grill (broil) or fry the sausages for 5 minutes until browned on
all sides.

Put the flour and salt into a mixing bowl and make a well in the
centre. Break in the eggs and gradually work in half the milk, beating
well until smooth. Beat in the rest of the milk.

Meanwhile, heat the oil in a large baking dish or roasting tin (pan)
in the oven until very hot. Place the sausages in the dish and pour
over the batter. Cook for 35-40 minutes until risen and puffy.
Serve at once.

This popular old-fashioned batter pudding was originally made with
lamb chops or slices of prime rump steak. Nowadays it is usually made
with sausages.

Suffolk fourses

25g/1 ounce fresh yeast
115g/4 ounces plus 1 teaspoon caster (superfine) sugar
300ml/1¼ cups warm milk
225g/2¼ sticks butter
900g/2 pounds strong plain (all-purpose) flour
½ teaspoon salt
115g/4 ounces dried fruit, (currants, raisins, etc.)
½ teaspoon mixed spice
3 eggs, beaten
Demerara (light brown cane) sugar for sprinkling

Cream the yeast with 1 teaspoon of the sugar and stir in the warm milk. Sift the flour and salt into a mixing bowl and rub in 50g/½ stick of butter until well combined, then add the sugar and dried fruit.

Melt the remaining butter and stir into the eggs, then pour into the yeast mixture, mixing well. Pour into the flour and mix with a round-bladed knife to make a light dough. Cover with cling film (plastic wrap) and leave in a warm place for about 2 hours, or until risen and doubled in size.

Knead the dough on a floured surface and roll out to a thickness of about 2cm/³/₄ inches and cut into 10cm/4-inch rounds. Place on greased baking trays and leave in a warm place for 30 minutes to rise.

Preheat the oven to 190°C/375°F/gas mark 5. When the dough has risen, sprinkle each round with sugar, mark into 4 sections and bake for 15-20 minutes, or until golden brown. Remove from the oven and cool on wire trays.

This would originally have been made using surplus dough from bread-making.

Oven bottom cake

15g/½ ounce fresh yeast
2½ teaspoons sugar
450-475ml/2-2⅛ cups warm water
675g/1½ pounds strong white bread flour
2 teaspoons salt
115g/1 stick butter, diced

Cream the yeast with the sugar and a little of the warm water and leave to stand until frothy. Sift the flour and salt into a large mixing bowl and pour in the yeast mixture and the remaining water. Mix to a smooth dough and turn out onto a floured surface. Knead until smooth and elastic, then put into a lightly oiled bowl, cover and leave to rise in a warm place until doubled in size.

Preheat the oven to 220°C/425°F/gas mark 7.

Grease a baking tray. Knock back the dough and knead lightly for 2-3 minutes. Knead the diced butter into the dough, pressing with your knuckles (the dough will be lumpy). Press out into a round and place on a greased baking sheet. Cover and leave to rise again.

Bake for 10 minutes, then reduce the heat to 190°C/375°F/gas mark 5 and bake for another 25-35 minutes. Cool on a wire rack.

In Yorkshire, this was made with surplus bread dough and eaten hot with butter and/or jam or preserves.

Lancashire bun cake

675g/1½ pounds strong white bread flour
15g/½ ounce salt
1x 7g/¼ ounce sachet Easy Blend (or other 'instant') yeast
50g/½ stick butter
300ml/1¼ cups warm milk
150ml/⅝ cup warm water
175g/6 ounces currants
75g/3 ounces raisins
75g/3 ounces sultanas (white raisins)
50g/2 ounces candied peel, chopped
1 teaspoon mixed spice

Put the flour, salt and yeast into a mixing bowl and rub in the butter. Pour in the milk and water and mix to a dough.

Turn out onto a floured surface and knead until smooth and elastic. Put the dough into a lightly oiled bowl and cover. Leave to rise in a warm place for 1½-2 hours, or until doubled in size.

Preheat the oven to 190°C/375°F/gas mark 5. Grease 2 x 450g/1-pound loaf tins (pans). Turn the dough onto a floured surface and knock back to remove all the air. Knead in the dried fruits, peel and spice and flatten to a rectangle. Roll up from the short end and put into the loaf tins. Cover and leave to rise in a warm place until doubled in size.

Bake for 30-35 minutes until cooked through. Remove from the oven and cool on a wire rack.

Lancacashire potato cakes

450g/1 pound peeled potatoes
30g/a generous ¼ stick butter
½ teaspoon salt
1 egg
115g/4 ounces plain (all-purpose) flour
1 teaspoon baking powder

Boil the potatoes until tender. Drain them and mash with the butter and salt. Add the rest of the ingredients to form a soft but not sticky dough and roll out to about 1.5cm/⅝-inch thickness and cut into rounds.

Cook for about 15 minutes on a hot greased griddle or well-greased frying pan, turning halfway through the cooking time. Serve at once with plenty of butter.

It's essential to use freshly boiled and mashed potatoes to ensure that the cooked potato cakes will be light and fluffy.

Caraway seed cake

175g/1¾ sticks butter
175g/6 ounces caster (superfine) sugar
2-4 teaspoons caraway seeds
3 eggs, separated
Large pinch of freshly grated nutmeg (optional)
225g/8 ounces self-raising (self-rising) flour
Milk to mix

Preheat the oven to 180°C/350°F/gas mark 4. Butter a 900g/
2-pound loaf tin (pan).

Cream the butter and sugar until pale and light and stir in the
caraway seeds. Whisk the egg whites until stiff but not dry and
gently beat in the egg yolks until well-blended.

Add to the creamed mixture with the spices, if using, and sift in
the flour, adding a little milk if necessary to achieve a soft
dropping consistency.

Pour into the loaf tin and smooth the top. Bake for just over an
hour until cooked through. Cool in the tin for 20 minutes, then
turn out onto a wire rack to cool completely.

*Often known as 'seed cake', this cake was very popular in days gone by and
appeared on many a Sunday tea table.*

Cinnamon and sultana flapjacks

150g/5½ ounces sultanas (white raisins)
100ml/scant ½ cup hot black tea
225g/2¼ sticks butter
225g/8 ounces light muscovado (soft light brown) sugar
150g/5½ ounces golden syrup (corn syrup)
350g/12 ounces rolled porridge oats
75g/3 ounces self-raising (self-rising) flour
2 teaspoons ground cinnamon

Preheat the oven to 180°C/350°F/gas mark 4. Lightly grease and line the base of a 23 x 30cm/9 x 12-inch rectangular cake tin (pan).

Place the sultanas in a bowl and pour the hot tea over, cover the bowl with cling film (plastic wrap) and leave to cool so that the sultanas soak up the tea and become plump.

Put the butter, sugar and syrup in a pan and heat gently, stirring until melted.

Put the oats in a bowl with the flour and cinnamon and stir in the sultanas. Make a well in the centre and pour in the butter mixture, mix thoroughly, then spoon into the prepared tin, pressing down well. Bake for 25-30 minutes, or until a deep golden around the edges but still soft in the centre. Remove from the oven, then mark into squares while hot.

You can also use any fruit tea, e.g. orange, mango and cinnamon, apple and ginger, rosehip, etc., instead of black tea, to impart an intriguing flavour.

Fresh lemonade

4 lemons
225g/8 ounces sugar
1.8 litres/7½ cups boiling water

Using a vegetable peeler, thinly pare the rind from the lemons, and then squeeze out the juice.

Put the lemon rind and sugar into a bowl and pour over the boiling water. Stir to dissolve the sugar, cover, and leave for 24 hours until completely cold.

Add the lemon juice (and more sugar if you wish) and strain into a jug. Chill until ready to serve. Serve with plenty of ice.

Homemade lemonade is a world away from the commercial variety. The sharp citrus burst of fresh lemons makes it a wonderfully refreshing drink.

MICHAELMAS

The Feast of Saint Michael the Archangel on September 29 is associated with the beginning of autumn and the shortening of days. In the past it was celebrated as Michaelmas Day and was one of the most important days of the year; by Michaelmas, the harvest had to be completed, and it was also a time for beginning new leases, settling accounts and paying dues.

A poem called the 'Posies of Gascoigne', published in 1575, mentioned this:

> *And when the tenauntes come*
> *to paie their quarter's rent,*
> *They bring some fowle at Midsummer,*
> *a dish of fish in Lent.*

Traditional foods for the day included plump roast goose (a 'stubble-goose': one that had fed well on the stubble of the fields after the harvest). By Michaelmas, the birds were in prime condition and tenants paid their rent with these plump, stubble geese. A popular saying stated that 'If you eat goose on Michaelmas Day you will never want money all the year round'. Legend has it that the custom of eating goose on Michaelmas day began because Queen Elizabeth I received the news of the defeat of the Spanish Armada, while she was eating a goose on Michaelmas Day, and that to commemorate the event she dined on goose on that day every year.

Autumn goose fairs were popular events, the most famous being the one held in Nottingham, which still survives today as a 'funfair' of the amusement-park variety. Thousands of geese were walked to the fair to be sold for the table.

In Ireland, Michaelmas Day was known as *Fombar na nGéan* ('The Goose Harvest'), and a plump roast goose took pride of place on the dinner table. In South Ulster and Munster, baked apples and jugs of cider accompanied the goose, because this was also the start of the apple harvest. Irish farming families slaughtered a sheep and gave a part of it to the poor in memory of the miracles of St Patrick through the assistance of St Michael. Michaelmas was a day of joy, plenty and celebration.

Special large loaves of bread were baked in some areas. On the Isle of Skye in Scotland, a procession around the church was held, and afterwards a special St Michael's bannock, the *struan Micheil*, was eaten. It was made with all the cereals grown on the farm during the year. Everyone, including any strangers, had to eat the bread that night to ensure the protection of St Michael.

Rosehips were gathered on Michaelmas Day in some parts of Yorkshire and made into a sweet drink; the day therefore became known as 'Hipping Day'.

Autumn fruits such as apples and pears have been enjoyed in England since time immemorial. Chaucer mentioned roast apples, cooked with sugar candy and *galingale*, a fragrant spice similar to ginger. Baked stuffed apples, apple pies and puddings, and of course, cider (applejack) are among the glories of English cuisine. Old-fashioned apple varieties such as Edmund's Pippin, Flower of Kent, Kidd's Orange and Ashmeads Kernel (first grown in 1700) are full of flavour, as are old-fashioned pear varieties such as Stinking Bishop and Green Huffcap.

Glossy, juicy blackberries are one of autumn's most delicious fruits. The purplish-black berries are known by various names in different regions: bramble, bumble-kit, bramble-kite, bly, brumme, brameberry, scaldhead and brambleberry are just some of the delightful country names. The berries grow on prickly bramble bushes and their inky juices stain fingers deep purple. The name of the bush is derived from *brambel*, or *brymbyl*, signifying 'prickly'.

In Scotland, blackberries are known as brambles, and in the Highlands the bush is called *an druise beannaichte*: 'the blessed bramble'. It was thought that Christ drove the moneylenders out of the temple with a bramble switch, and this is probably why the plant has been used as a protection against evil in the past.

It used to be considered unlucky to pick blackberries after a certain date. Usually around October 9, was the last time to gather the berries, as it was believed that on the next day the devil spat on every blackberry bush, thus making them poisonous to eat. This belief arose because October 10 was the feast of St Michael before the calendar was changed in 1752, and St Michael was responsible for throwing the devil out of heaven, where he is said to have landed in a blackberry bush!

It is true, though, that the juicy black berries start to be past their prime around this time of year, and are often oozing and overripe – and therefore indigestible.

Goose stuffed with black pudding and apples

1 x 4-5kg /8½-11 pounds oven-ready goose
375g/12 ounces black pudding, skin removed
1 goose liver
2 cloves garlic, finely chopped
3-4 cooking apples
5 tablespoons red wine
Salt and pepper
115g/4 ounces fresh white breadcrumbs

Preheat the oven to 200°C/400°F/gas mark 6.

Wipe the goose and remove any excess fat from inside. B reak up the black pudding in a bowl with a fork, removing any large pieces of white fat. Add the goose liver and ga rlic and beat until smooth. Peel and core the apples and chop finely. Add to the stuffing mixture with the wine and season to taste with salt and pepper. Mix very well and add the breadcrumbs.

Stuff the goose loosely with the mixture (don't overfill; the stuffing will swell during cooking). Cook any surplus stuffing separately in a greased dish. Secure the tail end with skewe rs and truss the goose neatly with string to hold the wings and legs close to the body. Prick the bird all over and sprinkle with salt and pepper.

Place on a rack in a roasting tin (pan) and cook for 30 minutes, then reduce the oven temperature to 180°C/350°F/gas mark 4 and cook for a further 3-3½ hours, or until cooked through. Leave to rest for at least 15 minutes before carving.

An oven-ready frozen goose should be thoroughly thawed slowly in the refrigerator before cooking. Prick the bird all over before roasting to allow the fat to escape, pouring off the accumulated fat from time to time during cooking.

Cider apple chicken with mushrooms

1 heaped tablespoon plain (all-purpose) flour
Salt and pepper
4 chicken legs or breasts
75g/¾ stick unsalted butter
2 tablespoons olive oil
225g/8 ounces button onions or shallots
500ml/2¼ cups dry cider (applejack)
225g/8 ounces button mushrooms
2 teaspoons Dijon mustard
150ml/⅝ cup crème fraîche
4 eating (dessert) apples
1 tablespoon caster (superfine) sugar
Chopped fresh parsley to garnish

Put the flour in a bowl, season well and use to coat the chicken
pieces. Shake off any excess. Heat 25g/¼ stick butter and 1
tablespoon oil in a large flameproof casserole. Add the onions, cook
until soft, then remove from the pan. Add the chicken pieces and
brown well on all sides. Add the cider, season to taste and bring to
the boil, stirring until thickened. Cook gently for 20-25 minutes.

Heat 25g/¼ stick butter in a frying pan and cook the mushrooms for
4 minutes. Add the cooked onions with the mushrooms and their
juices to the chicken and cook for 15 minutes. Adjust the seasoning
if necessary. Stir in the mustard and crème fraîche and heat through.

Melt the remaining butter in a frying pan. Core and slice the
apples and sauté them with the sugar until golden brown. Garnish
the chicken with the apples and sprinkle with chopped parsley.
Serve immediately.

*This delicious, creamy chicken dish garnished with caramelized apples makes
a striking main course.*

Cumberland sausage, apple and cider casserole

450g/1 pound Cumberland sausage (or other whole-hog pork sausage)
2 tablespoons oil or dripping
2 onions, sliced
3 large cooking apples
Salt and pepper to taste
300ml/1¼ cups cider (applejack)

Preheat the oven to 180°C/350°F/gas mark 4.

Heat the oil or dripping in a frying pan and lightly brown the sausage.

Peel, core and slice the apples into rings. Cut the sausage into 5cm/2-inch pieces and layer with the onions and apples in a casserole or baking dish. Season to taste and pour in the cider.

Cook for 40-45 minutes, or until the sausages are cooked through and the apples are tender. Serve with mashed potatoes and a green vegetable.

Cumberland sausage is wonderfully tasty and meaty, with the distinctive feature that it isn't twisted into links but made in one piece.

Autumn fruit crumble

675g/1½ pounds apples and pears, mixed (peeled weight)
Finely grated zest and juice of 1 orange
115g/4 ounces sugar
1 teaspoon ground cinnamon
Pinch ground mixed spice

For the crumble
75g/¾ stick butter
175g/6 ounces plain (all-purpose) flour
75g/3 ounces caster (superfine) sugar
1 teaspoon ground mixed spice
Pinch ground cloves

Preheat the oven to 200°C/400°F/gas mark 6.

Butter a large pie dish. Peel and core the fruit and cut into thick slices. Stir in the orange zest and juice, sugar and spices, mixing well. Put the mixture into the baking dish.

Rub the butter into the flour until the mixture resembles fine breadcrumbs, and then stir in the sugar and spices. Sprinkle evenly over the fruit and bake for about 30 minutes, or until golden brown. Serve with cream or custard.

Vary the fruits by using rhubarb, blackberries or plums instead of apples and pears.

Blackberry and apple crunch

4 tablespoons apple juice
450g/1 pound eating (dessert) apples, peeled
and sliced
½ teaspoon ground cinnamon
75g/¾ stick butter
175g/6 ounces wholemeal (whole-wheat)
breadcrumbs
50g/2 ounces roasted hazelnuts, chopped
4 tablespoons demerara (light brown cane) sugar
225g/8 ounces blackberries
Whole blackberries to decorate

Put the apple juice, apples and cinnamon in a pan and cook
gently until just soft, but still holding the shape of the fruit. Leave
to cool.

Heat the butter in a frying pan, add the breadcrumbs and cook
until golden brown and crisp. Leave to cool, and then stir in the
hazelnuts and sugar.

Divide half the apples and blackberries among four serving glasses
and cover with half the crunch mixture. Repeat the layers, finishing
with the crunch. Top each with a whole blackberry. Serve with
cream or ice cream.

*Do make sure that you pick only berries growing away from busy roads, as
those growing at the roadside will be contaminated with exhaust fumes. The
soft berries quickly become mushy and past their best, but will keep in the
refrigerator for a day. If the blackberries are rather tart, sprinkle them with
a little sugar first.*

Wardens (pears) in red wine

4 large firm pears
25g/1 ounce blanched almonds, halved
50g/2 ounces sugar
300ml/1¼ cups red wine
2 cloves
1 cinnamon stick, broken in half

Peel the pears, leaving the stalks intact. Stud the pears with the almond halves.

Put the sugar, wine, cloves and halved cinnamon stick in a saucepan just large enough to hold the pears and heat gently until the sugar has dissolved.

Add the pears, standing them upright, and cover the pan. Simmer gently for about 20 minutes, or until the pears are tender (the exact time depends on the ripeness of the pears), basting from time to time with the liquid. Remove the pears to a serving dish using a slotted spoon.

Boil the remaining liquid in the pan until thick and syrupy. Remove the cloves and cinnamon and pour the liquid over the pears. Serve warm or cold with whipped cream.

This dish originated in the West Country and would originally have been made using cider (applejack); you can use this instead of wine if you prefer. Pears used to be called 'wardens' or 'wardons', which may be from the Bedfordshire town of the same name, or it could also be named after Wardon Abbey, where pears were cultivated there by Cistercian monks.

Quince jelly

1.75 kg / 3½ pounds quinces
3.4 litres / about 3½ quarts water
1.2 kg / 2 pounds 10 ounces sugar

Wash the quinces and scrub away the greyish down. Chop the fruit roughly and place in a large pan with 2.75 litres/almost 3 quarts water. Cover and simmer over a low heat for about 1 hour, or until the fruit is soft: the time depends on the ripeness of the fruit. When soft, press the fruit with the back of a wooden spoon. Ladle the fruit and juice into a scalded jelly bag; leave to drip for 30 minutes.

Remove the pulp from the bag and return to the pan with the remaining water. Simmer for 30 minutes, then ladle back into the jelly bag for a second straining.

Measure all the juice into the rinsed-out pan; for every 600ml/ 2½ cups of juice, add 450g/1 pound granulated sugar. Cook over a low heat, stirring, until the sugar has dissolved, then bring to the boil and boil rapidly for 10 minutes.

Remove from the heat and test for a set. Skim off any scum with a metal spoon and pour into warm, sterilized jars. Cover with wax discs and leave to cool completely before sealing with a lid or cellophane cover.

Quinces are inedible when raw but have a delightful flavour when cooked. The raw fruit is very hard, with a yellowish-green skin that is covered with down. The flesh turns deep-pink when cooked. As this jelly cooks, it will fill the house with a wonderful fragrance. Add a spoonful to apple pies or crumbles before cooking, or serve with roast meats and game.

Dumpsie dearie jam (preserves)

900g/2 pounds pears
900g/2 pounds cooking apples
900g/2 pounds plums
Grated zest and juice of 1 lemon
Pinch of ground cloves
12g/½ ounce fresh ginger root, bruised
2.25kg/5 pounds sugar

Peel and core the pears and apples. Halve and stone the plums.
Put all the fruit into a large pan with the lemon zest, juice, ground
cloves and bruised ginger root. Simmer very gently until the fruit
is soft; if it starts to stick to the pan add a little water.

Stir in the sugar until completely dissolved, then bring to the boil.
Boil rapidly for about 15-20 minutes, or until setting point has
been reached.

Pour into warm sterilized jars, cover and seal.

An old country recipe from Gloucestershire which
uses windfall apples, pears and plums.

NB: Jars and bottles must be sterilized and
warmed before filling them to the brim to allow for
shrinkage. Wash the jars/bottles in hot, soapy
water, rinse and put in a low oven to dry and
become warm. Wipe the outside of the filled
jars/bottles and seal tightly with lids.

Blackberry butter

1 kg/2¼ pounds blackberries
1 kg/2¼ pounds cooking apples
Grated zest and juice of 2 lemons
350g/12 ounces sugar to every 450g/1 pound fruit pulp

Wash the fruit and chop the apples roughly; there's no need to core and peel them. Place the blackberries and apples in a pan with the lemon zest and juice and simmer gently for about 15 minutes, or until very soft.

Push the mixture through a sieve and weigh the pulp. Stir in the required amount of sugar and heat gently until the sugar has dissolved completely. Bring to the boil and cook gently until the mixture is thick and creamy, stirring all the time – about 20 minutes depending on the ripeness of the fruit.

Pour into warm, sterilized jars and cover with plastic or metal lids.

A beautifully deep-coloured spread that's delicious with scones and cream or as a filling for a plain sponge cake.

NB: Jars and bottles must be sterilized and warmed before filling them to the brim to allow for shrinkage. Wash the jars/bottles in hot, soapy water, rinse and put in a low oven to dry and become warm. Wipe the outside of the filled jars/bottles and seal tightly with lids.

Pickled plums

450g/1 pound small plums
300ml/1¼ cups white
distilled vinegar
225g/8 ounces sugar
Finely pared rind of ½ lemon
A small piece fresh root
ginger, bruised
4 whole cloves
1 cinnamon stick

Wash and dry the plums and
remove the stalks. Prick the
fruit all over with a darning needle and place in a pan. Cover with
vinegar and add the sugar.

Tie the lemon rind and spices in a piece of muslin and add to the
pan. Heat gently, stirring, until the sugar has dissolved completely,
then bring to the boil. Reduce the heat and simmer very gently
until the fruit is tender; be careful not to let the skins break.

Remove the fruit with a perforated spoon and pack into warm,
sterilized jars. Discard the muslin and boil the liquid rapidly for 5
minutes, then pour immediately over the plums and cover the jars
at once. Keep for at least 1 month before eating.

*These are delicious with cold meat and game pies as well as cold meats and
poultry. You can use small red plums, damsons or greengages in this recipe.*

*NB: Jars and bottles must be sterilized and warmed before filling them to the
brim to allow for shrinkage. Wash the jars/bottles in hot, soapy water, rinse
and put in a low oven to dry and become warm. Wipe the outside of the
filled jars/bottles and seal tightly with lids.*

Cider toffee apple cake

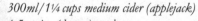

300ml/1¼ cups medium cider (applejack)
4-5 eating (dessert) apples
200g/7 ounces light muscovado (soft light brown) sugar
150g/1½ sticks butter
115g/4 ounces golden caster (golden superfine or baker's) sugar
2 eggs, beaten
225g/8 ounces plain (all-purpose) flour
1 teaspoon baking powder

Preheat the oven to 190°C/375°F/gas mark 5.
Butter a 20cm/8-inch round non-stick cake tin (pan;
not loose-based) or line a 20cm/8-inch tin with non-
stick baking paper.

In a small pan, heat the cider until boiling, then
lower the heat and simmer gently until reduced by half. Remove
from the heat and leave until cold.

Peel and core the apples and cut into thick slices. Heat 25g/¼ stick
butter and the light muscovado sugar in a pan until melted,
stirring occasionally. Bring to the boil and allow to bubble for a
minute or two to a golden caramel. Pour onto the base of the
prepared tin. Arrange the sliced apples on top of the caramel.

Cream the rest of the butter and golden caster sugar until light
and gradually beat in the eggs. Sift in the flour and baking powder
and fold in carefully until well-mixed. Gently stir in the cold cider.

Spoon the mixture over the apples and bake for 25-35 minutes
until cooked through. Remove from the oven and allow to cool
slightly for a few minutes, and then turn out onto a serving plate,
so that the apples are on top. Serve warm.

Scottish bramble cake

115g/1 stick butter
115g/4 ounces caster (superfine) sugar
1 egg
225g/8 ounces plain (all-purpose) flour
2 teaspoons baking powder
Pinch salt
150ml/⅝ cup milk

For the topping
50g/½ stick butter
115g/4 ounces unrefined demerara (light brown cane) sugar
50g/2 ounces flour
1 teaspoon mixed spice
225g/8 ounces blackberries

Preheat the oven to 180°C/350°F/gas mark 4. Butter an 18 x 28cm/7 x 11-inch cake tin (pan).

Cream the butter and sugar in a mixing bowl until light, then beat in the egg. Sift the flour and baking powder into the mixture and stir in the salt, mixing well. Add sufficient milk to make a smooth batter and pour into the prepared tin.

Cream the butter and sugar for the topping and work in the flour and spice to make a crumble. Sprinkle the berries on top of the cake, then top with the crumble mixture. Bake for about 40-60 minutes, or until the topping is golden brown. Serve warm or cold with thick cream or custard.

A lovely cake for teatime that can also be served as a pudding (dessert).

HALLOWEEN

The eve of the Feast of All Saints (in the past called All Hallows) on October 31 is known as Halloween. In the past, Halloween was widely believed to be the time when the spirits of the dead appeared and witches gathered. Superstitious country folk took every precaution to protect themselves and their animals from the evil influences of witches, goblins, evil spirits and demons on this night: church bells were rung, bonfires lit and prayers for the dead offered. In the past, bonfires were lit to frighten off evil spirits; over the centuries the fires were gradually replaced with hollowed out turnips or pumpkin lanterns, with a lighted candle inside, placed on gateposts – the origin of pumpkin lanterns today.

Fortune telling and magic, shrouded in mystery, were other traditional customs of Halloween. In Scotland a 'fortune telling pudding', (usually a bowl of *cranachan*) containing small charms was placed on the table. Each charm had a specific meaning, and a person with 'second sight' would interpret this to the recipient of the charm. A coin, for instance, meant wealth for the coming year; a ring was a sign that marriage was imminent, while a thimble meant that the finder was destined to remain single.

Ritual games and divination using apples, nuts and candles were practised. Several counties in England and Scotland combined Halloween with Mischief Night, when children played practical jokes on their neighbours.

In fishing regions of Scotland, the priest or minister blessed the nets and prayed for successful catches. Bonfires were lit to ward off evil spirits, lucky charms protected against evil, and masks were worn to avoid being recognized by the spirits – Halloween 'guising' is a remnant of those beliefs. The charms were incorporated into cakes and puddings.

Throughout Britain, all sorts of specially baked cakes and gingerbreads were – and indeed still are – enjoyed at this time of year. The custom is derived from the pagan practice of baking special cakes to celebrate the onset of winter. Gingerbreads were especially popular, particularly in Scotland. Northern areas also enjoyed gingerbread made with luxury ingredients such as treacle (molasses), honey and spices to make a really special festive cake. 'Parkin pigs' were sold at the October Fair in Bingley, West Yorkshire; in other parts of the West Riding of Yorkshire, 'Parkin Sunday' was a November festival. The feast of All Saints on November 1 was known as 'Cake Night' in Ripon and 'Caking Day' in Sheffield, when boys dressed as mummers went around the farmhouses collecting money to buy parkin: a dense, solid gingerbread made with oatmeal.

Until the Reformation, it was customary for poor people to go from house to house begging for 'soul cakes' in return for prayers for the souls of the departed, and every housewife had a batch ready for the callers. In Lancashire, small, flat spiced buns were popular, while in Yorkshire the buns were fruited as well as spiced. In Northamptonshire caraway seeds were included in the buns. Often soul cakes were sent as a gift to the relatives of a deceased person. In Cheshire, children called at houses singing the 'souling song' and were sometimes accompanied by musicians.

> *Soul! Soul! For a Soul Cake,*
> *I pray you good missis, a Soul Cake*

The 'souling' ceremony was known as 'hodening', where a man dressed in a long cloak carried a wooden horse's head on a pole (rather like a hobbyhorse); the head had hinged jaws which snapped fiercely at the watching crowds.

As time passed, the custom of souling died out and the cakes were replaced by gifts of money or sweets, culminating in the modern custom of 'trick or treat.'

Spicy pumpkin soup

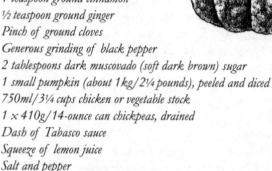

2 tablespoons olive oil
1 large onion, chopped
2 cloves garlic, chopped
½ teaspoon ground cumin
1 teaspoon ground cinnamon
½ teaspoon ground ginger
Pinch of ground cloves
Generous grinding of black pepper
2 tablespoons dark muscovado (soft dark brown) sugar
1 small pumpkin (about 1kg/2¼ pounds), peeled and diced
750ml/3¼ cups chicken or vegetable stock
1 x 410g/14-ounce can chickpeas, drained
Dash of Tabasco sauce
Squeeze of lemon juice
Salt and pepper
Cayenne pepper to finish (optional)

Heat the oil in a large pan and add the onion and garlic. Cook gently for 2-3 minutes until beginning to soften, then add the spices, sugar and pumpkin. Cook for 5 minutes, stirring until fragrant. Pour in the stock and bring to the boil.

Simmer gently until the pumpkin is tender. Add the chickpeas, Tabasco and lemon juice. Taste and adjust the seasoning if needed.

Purée the mixture in a food processor or with a hand-held blender until smooth. Serve piping hot, with a sprinkling of cayenne if liked.

A tasty, warming soup for Halloween.

Barbecue beans

300g/10½ ounces haricot (navy) beans, soaked overnight
400ml/1¾ cups water
2 tablespoons oil
1 onion, finely chopped
1-2 garlic cloves, crushed
4 tablespoons black treacle (molasses)
2 teaspoons wholegrain mustard
1 dessertspoon tomato purée
1 tablespoon Worcestershire sauce
110ml/scant ½ cup white wine or cider vinegar
150g/5½ ounces tomato passata (sieved tomatoes)
1 teaspoon cayenne pepper
Pinch salt
1 tablespoon cornflour (cornstarch)

Put the soaked beans and water into a large pan and bring to the boil. Cover and simmer gently for 30 minutes until tender – add more water if necessary. Drain, reserving the cooking liquor.

Heat the oil and cook the onion and garlic for a few minutes until soft but not browned. Add the sugar, mustard, tomato purée and Worcestershire sauce, stirring well. Cook over a low heat for 5 minutes, then add the beans, vinegar, tomato passata, cayenne and salt.

Blend the cornflour with a little of the reserved liquor and stir into the bean mixture with the remaining cooking liquor. Bring to the boil and simmer for 20-30 minutes, stirring from time to time until the beans are tender.

Serve these tasty beans with hunks of crusty bread to mop up the sauce.

Broomstick bangers

8 large unpeeled baking potatoes
50g/½ stick butter
2 tablespoons oil
2 onions, sliced
8 Frankfurter sausages
Salt

Preheat the oven to 170°C/350°/gas mark 3.

Wash the potatoes and dry well. Rub the skins with butter and place on a baking tray. Bake for 2 hours, or until soft.

Heat the oil in a frying pan and cook the onions until soft and golden. Add the sausages to the pan until heated through. Make a deep cut in each potato, sprinkle with salt and place a sausage and a spoonful of onions in each one. Serve immediately with mustard.

Children (and adults) will love this piping-hot sausage, onion and potato combination. The sausages stick out from the potatoes to resemble broomsticks.

Onion marmalade

900g/2 pounds onions, sliced thinly into rings
150ml/⅝ cup red wine
1 tablespoon whole-grain mustard
2 tablespoons red wine vinegar
2 tablespoons unrefined demerara (light brown cane) sugar
2 cloves garlic, crushed
Salt and pepper

Separate the onion rings and place in a large frying pan with the rest of the ingredients over a moderate heat. Bring to the boil, stir well, cover and simmer gently for 30-45 minutes, or until the onions are soft.

Remove the lid; increase the heat and cook, stirring occasionally until the mixture is brown and thick.

This tasty relish is excellent with the Broomstick bangers and hot dogs. Spoon into split hot-dog rolls and pop a hot cooked sausage on top.

Colcannon

450g/1 pound mashed potatoes
450g/1 pound cooked cabbage, chopped
Salt and pepper
75g/¾ stick butter
1 onion, chopped
Milk if needed

Mix the potatoes and cabbage and season with salt and pepper.
Melt half the butter in a frying pan and cook the onion until soft.
Remove the onion from the pan and add to the potato and
cabbage mixture. Add a little milk if the mixture is very stiff.

Heat the remaining butter in the pan and when hot, add the mixture,
spreading it out in the pan. Cook until brown, then cut it roughly,
continuing to cook until brown and crisp.

*A popular Irish Halloween dish. A ring was sometimes concealed in the dish
and the person who found it would be married within the year.*

Irish barm brack

225g/8 ounces mixed dried fruit
150g/5½ ounces dark muscovado (dark soft brown) sugar
300ml/1¼ cups Irish stout (or other dark beer)
2 eggs, beaten
300g/10½ ounces self-raising (self-rising) flour
1 teaspoon mixed spice
1 teaspoon ground ginger

Mix the dried fruit, sugar and stout in a bowl. Cover and leave to stand for a few hours or overnight.

Preheat the oven to 180°C/350°F/gas mark 4. Grease and line a 900g (2-pound) loaf tin (pan).

Beat the eggs into the fruit mixture, followed by the flour and spices, mixing well. Pour into the loaf tin and bake for 50-60 minutes, or until cooked through. Leave to cool in the tin.

Turn out when cold and wrap in greaseproof (waxed) paper. Store in an airtight for 2 days before eating to develop the flavour.

A moist, fruity tea-bread, which has been enjoyed in Ireland for hundreds of years. Symbolic charms were often included, such as a ring or a thimble. Nowadays only the ring is included by commercial bakers.

Parkin

225g/2¼ sticks butter
175g/6 ounces dark muscovado (soft dark brown) sugar
115g/4 ounces black treacle (molasses)
115g/4 ounces golden syrup (corn syrup)
450g/1 pound plain (all-purpose) flour
1 teaspoon bicarbonate of soda (baking soda)
1 tablespoon ground ginger
350g/12 ounces medium oatmeal
3 eggs, beaten

Preheat the oven to 180°C/350°F/gas mark 4. Grease a Yorkshire pudding tin (patty pan) or roasting tin (pan).

In a saucepan, melt together the butter, sugar, treacle and golden syrup, but do not allow the mixture to become hot. Stir together the dry ingredients in a large mixing bowl and gradually add the melted butter mixture. Stir in the eggs and mix thoroughly.

Pour into the tin and cook for 45 minutes to 1 hour. Remove from the oven and cool in the tin.

Store in an airtight tin for at least 3 days before cutting. Parkin will keep well stored in an airtight tin for up to 2 weeks.

There are many different kinds of parkin in the north of England. This old-fashioned recipe results in a wonderfully moist, soft and sticky parkin, fragrant with ginger.

Fresh ginger gingerbread

425g/15 ounces plain (all-purpose) flour
¼ teaspoon salt
1 tablespoon grated fresh ginger root
1 tablespoon finely grated orange zest
1 teaspoon ground cinnamon
Pinch ground cloves
115g/4 ounces molasses sugar (soft dark brown sugar)
2 eggs
1½ teaspoons bicarbonate of soda (baking soda)
250ml/1⅛ cup molasses
115g/1 stick unsalted butter
225ml/1 cup hot water
2 tablespoons unrefined demerara (light brown cane) sugar

Preheat the oven to 180°C/350°F/gas mark 4. Grease and line a
23cm/9-inch square tin.

Sift the flour, salt bicarbonate of soda, cinnamon and cloves into
a bowl. Cream the butter and sugar until blended and creamy.
Beat in the treacle, followed by the eggs.

Gradually beat in the flour mixture, alternately with the hot water,
mixing well. Stir in the grated fresh ginger. Pour into the tin and
sprinkle the demerara sugar over the top. Bake for 35-40 minutes
until cooked through. Cool in the tin for 5 minutes, then finish
cooling on a wire rack.

Moist, soft and delectable, this is made with fresh root, not ground, ginger,
and contains molasses and orange zest.

Fortune telling crowdie

175g/6 ounces oatmeal
300ml/1¼ cups double (heavy) cream
3 tablespoons honey (heather honey is best)
2 tablespoons whisky
175g/6 ounces raspberries (optional)

Toast the oatmeal in a dry frying pan over a high heat until lightly browned. Allow to cool.

Whip the cream until thickened but not stiff (the oatmeal will thicken the cream even more) and stir in the oatmeal and honey. Slowly stir in the whisky and raspberries and spoon into small serving glasses. Chill until ready to serve.

This luxurious dessert is an ancient Scottish speciality and is very rich and alcoholic! The raspberries aren't traditional, but they make it extra-special.

Irish apple dumplings

450g/1 pound shortcrust (medium-flake) pastry
50g/½ stick butter
4 tablespoons light muscovado (soft light brown) sugar
1 teaspoon ground cinnamon (optional)
6 apples, peeled and cored
6 cloves
Milk to glaze

Preheat the oven to 200°C/400°F/gas mark 6. Grease a large baking tray.

Roll out the pastry on a floured surface and cut into 6 rounds. Cream the butter and sugar until soft and add the cinnamon if using.

Fill each apple with a little of the mixture and top with a clove. Place each apple on a pastry round and dampen the edges of the pastry with a little milk. Draw up the edges and press well together. Place, sealed-side down, on the baking tray and brush with milk. Bake for about 30 minutes; the exact cooking time depends on the ripeness of the apples.

Serve with whipped cream or ice cream.

A favourite Irish treat, especially when served after a light main course.

Wizard pudding

(Bradford Family Recipe)

115g/1 stick butter
115g/4 ounces demerara (light brown cane) sugar
2 eggs, separated
115g/4 ounces plain (all-purpose) flour
1 teaspoon bicarbonate of soda (baking soda)
1-2 tablespoons raspberry jam or preserves

Grease a medium pudding basin (heatproof bowl).

Cream the butter and sugar together until light and creamy. Beat in the egg yolks until well mixed. Sift in the flour and bicarbonate of soda. Whisk the egg whites until stiff and gently fold into the mixture until incorporated. Spoon the jam (preserves) into the base of the greased pudding basin and spoon the mixture on top. Cover and steam for 1½ hours. Turn out and serve with custard.

Could this have been called Wizard Pudding because it miraculously disappeared so quickly, or was there some other reason? Sadly the explanation seems to have been lost, if there ever was one in the first place…

Few people seem to have the time or the inclination these days to make their own steamed puddings; instead they are more likely to buy them from the supermarket and microwave them. Yet they are remarkably easy to prepare and cook, and somehow manage to taste completely different when they are turned out and eaten immediately – especially if they are served with 'proper custard'. RB

Toffee bread pudding

(Bradford Family Recipe)

750g/1 pound 10 ounces bread
Few drops vanilla extract
Milk
115g/1 stick butter
225g/8 ounces golden syrup (corn syrup)
225g/8 ounces unrefined demerara (light brown cane) sugar

Cut the bread into 1cm/½-inch squares and place in a bowl.
Combine the vanilla with the milk and pour over enough to soak
the bread, but the mixture must not be sodden.

Heat the butter, syrup and sugar in a medium saucepan until the
sugar has dissolved completely. Bring to the boil and cook to a
golden-brown caramel. Add the soaked bread squares and boil for
1 minute. Serve immediately with whipped cream.

If you take into consideration the fact that the now-ubiquitous sticky toffee
pudding – a dish every English restaurant has to have on its menu these days
– had not yet been invented by Francis Coulson at Sharrow Bay, then this
was a highly original dish. It could be considered a bit of a dietician's
nightmare, and it makes me wonder how, as a family, we managed to retain
any sort of sensible waistline. RB

Candied pumpkin slices

225g/8 ounces sugar
150ml/⅝ cup water
1kg/2¼ pounds (approximate weight) pumpkin flesh, cut into thick slices,
* about 5cm/2 inches in length*
Ground cinnamon for sprinkling

Put the sugar and water into a large frying pan and heat gently
until the sugar has dissolved completely. Add the pumpkin slices,
cover the pan and cook gently over a very low heat for 1 hour, or
until the pumpkin is tender. Remove the lid towards the end of
the cooking time to allow the liquid to become syrupy and coat
the slices.

Place the pumpkin slices on a serving plate and chill until ready to
serve. Sprinkle with ground cinnamon just before serving.

*If you're buying a pumpkin to make a Halloween jack-o'-lantern, you can
use the flesh in this unusual but delicious recipe.*

Witches' hats

10 round plain biscuits (cookies)
2 tablespoons apricot jam or preserves
10 marshmallows
115g/4 ounces plain (dark) chocolate
1 teaspoon sunflower oil
25g/1 ounce sugar
2 tablespoons water

Spread a little jam or preserves on the centre of each biscuit. Stick a marshmallow on each, wide-end downwards, and place on a wire rack.

Put the chocolate, oil, sugar and water into a small pan over a low heat, stirring until melted and smooth. Set aside to cool and thicken. Spoon over each biscuit and marshmallow until completely coated. Leave to set.

Children will enjoy making these deliciously spooky party treats.

Hot spiced cider

1.7 litres/7 cups cider (either applejack or non-alcoholic apple cider)
4 whole cloves
1 teaspoon grated nutmeg
½ teaspoon ground ginger
3 allspice berries, lightly crushed
1 cinnamon stick, broken
2 tablespoons dark muscovado (soft dark brown) sugar

Heat the cider with the spices and sugar in a large pan over a low heat until very hot – but don't allow the mixture to boil.

Strain into a warm serving bowl and serve in heated cups or glasses.

This spicy drink is wonderfully warming on a chilly autumn night.

THANKSGIVING

Thanksgiving Day is celebrated throughout the USA on the fourth Thursday in November and is a national public holiday. Families try to be together for the celebration, often travelling great distances to get home. People invite friends or neighbours who would otherwise be alone to join them for the meal. The table is laden with plenty of food, which always includes the traditional foods of the 'first thanksgiving feast'. As Americans sit down to their annual Thanksgiving dinner, they remember the first Pilgrims to arrive in the New World in 1620.

On their arrival, the Pilgrims were faced with new, strange foods, and without the help and advice of the Native American Indians, they would have starved. The Indians taught the Pilgrims how to live off the indigenous plants, berries, birds, fish and game. Many of the first settlers died due to the bad conditions, and when the harvest was finally gathered in, Governor William Bradford was so relieved he ordered a three-day feast of Thanksgiving.

The devout Pilgrims gave thanks to God for their survival and celebrated their first harvest in 1621 with an enormous outdoor feast. Among the invited guests were 90 Wampanoag Indians and their chief, Massasoit, who brought gifts of food. This first meal has become the model for today's Thanksgiving meal. Turkey, cranberries, sweet potatoes, corn-on-the-cob and pumpkin are all included in the traditional dinner, just as they were in the original pilgrims' feast, along with ducks, geese, deer, fish and shellfish.

'Indian corn' became a mainstay of the settlers. It was grilled, boiled, roasted, pounded, ground and made into small cakes and bread, as well as a delicious pudding made from cornmeal, molasses, milk and spices, known as 'Indian pudding'. Corn was also part of the first clambakes, which remain a famous traditional New England speciality. The Indians showed the Pilgrims how to build a fire in a rock-lined pit on the beach, add more rocks, then a layer of seaweed, followed by the food to be cooked – lobsters, clams, mussels, etc. More seaweed was then packed around the food, which was kept steaming by topping up with seawater.

Pumpkins were made into soup, baked or stewed and served as a vegetable, or cooked in a rich, sweet pie. Pumpkin flesh was mixed with spices to make delicious pies, which were very popular.

Blueberries and cranberries were used in both sweet and savoury dishes, particularly sweet pies. The Native American Indians dried and powdered wild blueberries and rubbed the powder into venison meat before smoking it over a wood fire.

All types of squash are hugely popular in the USA, where since ancient times they have been invaluable to Native Americans who, as well as eating the flesh, dried the hard outer shells and used them as drinking cups and bowls and also made musical instruments from them. The word 'squash' actually comes from the Native American word *askutasquash* which means 'eaten raw', although they must be cooked before eating.

Native Americans collected cranberries from the many cranberry bogs to use as food and medicine (wounds were bathed in cranberry juice) and also used them to dye feathers and cloth. The tart, scarlet berries were called 'craneberries' or 'bounce berries' by the Pilgrims. Cranberries were tested for freshness by their ability to bounce when thrown.

Native American and Canadian First Nations people made maple sugar and syrup long before the arrival of white settlers, and the process has changed little since then. In early spring, they pierced the tree trunks with tomahawks and placed a wood chip under the hole to channel the sap into a bark receptacle. They boiled the sap in clay containers over fires protected by a roof of tree branches (a type of early sugar-house) to obtain maple sugar. When the boiled syrup was about to granulate in its final boil-down, it was poured into a trough made from a smoothed-out log, then stirred and rubbed with into sugar grains (maple sugar) known as *ziinzibaakwad* in Ojibwe. Warm sugar was poured from the trough into *makuks* (containers) of birch bark. This was a staple seasoning and an important year-round food, eaten with grains, fish, fruits and vegetables. In summer, it was dissolved in water to make a refreshing, cooling drink. In winter it was stirred into various roots, leaf and bark teas. Maple sugar was so important that its name was given by the Ojibwe to the month (late March-April, in northern Minnesota) when sugaring took place: *iskigamizige giizis*, the sap-boiling moon (month).

Early European explorers were astonished by this 'Indian sugar'. A British Royal Society paper written in 1685 records, 'The Savages of Canada, in the time that the sap rises, in the Maple, make an incision in the Tree, by which it runs out; and after they have evaporated eight pounds of the liquor, there remains one pound...'

This early version of the 'sugar-shack' gradually evolved over the years, until today the sugar-shack is not only a place where maple syrup is produced, but also a place for friends to meet and enjoy a traditional meal. Clouds of sweet, fragrant steam from the boilers mingle with the enticing aroma of hot maple syrup in the crisp, cold winter air to awaken appetites. Many sugar-houses are open to the public during the boiling season, and some have restaurants serving delicious pancakes with freshly made maple syrup.

Creamed corn soup

25g/¼ stick butter
1 onion, finely diced
1 potato, peeled and cubed
1 x 425g/1-pound can creamed sweetcorn (corn)
300ml/1¼ cups chicken stock
Salt and white pepper
Single (light) cream
Freshly chopped chives

Melt the butter and fry the onions until soft and translucent. Add the potato and cook until slightly soft. Pour in the creamed sweetcorn and stock, stir well and bring to the boil. Cover and simmer for 30 minutes, or until the vegetables are cooked.

In a food processor or blender, process until smooth, then pass through a sieve. Season to taste. Garnish with swirls of cream and chopped chives.

This creamy corn soup makes an ideal first course for the Thanksgiving meal.

Perfect roast turkey

2.7-6.3kg/6-14-pound fresh turkey
Salt and pepper
Butter or olive oil
150ml/⅝ cup water

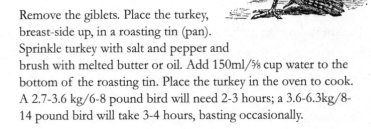

Preheat the oven to
170°C/350°F/gas mark 3.

Remove the giblets. Place the turkey,
breast-side up, in a roasting tin (pan).
Sprinkle turkey with salt and pepper and
brush with melted butter or oil. Add 150ml/⅝ cup water to the
bottom of the roasting tin. Place the turkey in the oven to cook.
A 2.7-3.6 kg/6-8 pound bird will need 2-3 hours; a 3.6-6.3kg/8-
14 pound bird will take 3-4 hours, basting occasionally.

If the turkey is becoming too brown before it is cooked, loosely
cover it with foil and continue cooking. Make sure that the turkey
is cooked – pierce the thigh, and if the juices run clear with no
trace of pink, it is ready.

Remove the bird from the oven, and allow it to stand for 20
minutes before serving. This allows the juices to redistribute for
easier carving.

*A glistening, golden roast turkey is the hallowed centrepiece of the traditional
Thanksgiving dinner. Stuffing has been prepared separately (see Pork and
pecan stuffing, page 216) to allow a shorter cooking time for the turkey itself.
Also, UK Government guidelines currently advise not to stuff the body of
the bird, to avoid the possibility of contracting salmonella.*

Pork and pecan stuffing

25g/¼ stick butter
2 tablespoons finely chopped onion
115g/4 ounces fresh white or brown breadcrumbs
450g/1 pound pork sausage meat
4 tablespoons pecans, chopped
1 teaspoon chopped thyme
1 teaspoon finely chopped sage
Salt and pepper to taste

Preheat the oven to 200°C/400°F/gas mark 6.

Melt the butter and cook the onion until soft and transparent.
Tip into a bowl and stir in the rest of the ingredients, mixing well.
Shape into 12 balls and place on a greased baking tray. Bake for
25 minutes, until golden brown.

Serve with the roast turkey on page 215.

A tasty, nutty stuffing that's delicious with roast turkey.

Autumn fruit-stuffed squash

4 acorn squash, halved, with seeds and fibres removed
2 tablespoons oil
1 onion, finely chopped
2 cooking apples, peeled, cored and chopped
75g/3 ounces dried pears, chopped
4 tablespoons apple juice
1 tablespoon dark muscovado (soft dark brown) sugar
Pinch each of ground cinnamon, cloves and ginger
75g/3 ounces pecans or walnuts
Salt and pepper

Preheat the oven to 180°C/350°F/gas mark 4.

Put the squash, cut-side down, in a lightly oiled baking tin (pan) and pour in a little water. Bake for about 30 minutes until just tender.

Heat the oil and gently fry the onions until soft but not brown. Stir in the apples, pears, juice, sugar and spices. Season to taste and bring to the boil, stirring. Simmer gently for a few minutes, then remove from the heat and add the pecans.

Turn the squash halves over and season the insides with salt and pepper. Spoon some of the filling into each hollow and bake for another 15-20 minutes, or until the filling is hot and bubbling.

This tasty recipe makes a flavoursome vegetarian main course or vegetable accompaniment.

Baked sweet potatoes and apples

675g/1½ pounds pink sweet potatoes, peeled
½ teaspoon salt
4 eating (dessert) apples
1 tablespoon lemon juice
Pinch of ground cinnamon
50g/½ stick butter
125ml/½ cup apple juice or cider (applejack)
1 tablespoon light muscovado (soft light brown) sugar

Preheat the oven to 180°C/350°F/gas mark 4.
Butter a 900ml/1 quart (approx.) ovenproof dish.

Cut the sweet potatoes into 1.5cm/⅝-inch slices
and place in a pan of boiling water with the salt.
Cook for 8-10 minutes until almost tender, then drain.
Cut the apples into small dice and blend with the
lemon juice and cinnamon. Arrange half the sweet
potatoes in the base of the dish and cover with the apples, then
add the rest of the potatoes.

Heat together the butter, apple juice or cider and sugar until the
butter has melted. Pour the mixture over the potatoes and bake
for about 45 minutes until tender.

The flavours of sweet potatoes and apples complement each other well and are
excellent with roast meat and poultry.

Cranberry and pecan tart

<u>For the pastry</u>
110g/1 stick butter, diced
175g/6 ounces plain (all-purpose) flour
2 tablespoons icing (confectioner's) sugar
Pinch of salt
1 large egg yolk, beaten with 1¼ tablespoons water

<u>For the filling</u>
3 large eggs
225g/8 ounces light muscovado (soft light brown) sugar
150ml/⅝ cup golden syrup (corn syrup)
50g/½ stick butter
1 teaspoon vanilla extract
175g/6 ounces cranberries
115g/4 ounces pecans, roughly chopped

Preheat the oven to 180°C/350°F/gas mark 4. Lightly grease a
23-25cm/9-10-inch flan tin or pie dish.

Rub the butter into the flour until the mixture resembles
breadcrumbs; this can be done in a food processor. Stir in the
sugar and salt, then add the egg yolk and water and mix or
process until the mixture binds together. Wrap in cling film
(plastic wrap) and chill for an hour.

Meanwhile, to make the filling, whisk the eggs, sugar, golden
syrup, butter and vanilla until smooth. Stir in the cranberries and
pecans. Roll out the dough about 1cm/½-inch thick and line the
tin. Pour the filling into the pastry case and bake for 40-45 minutes
until golden. Cool in the tin, then finish cooling on a wire rack.

Juicy, tart cranberries, crunchy pecans and syrup are a winning combination.

'Impossible' coconut pie

4 eggs
55g/½ stick butter
175g/6 ounces sugar
75g/3 ounces plain (all-purpose) flour
Pinch salt
½ teaspoon baking powder
425ml/2 scant cups milk
115g/4 ounces desiccated (shredded) coconut
1 teaspoon vanilla extract

Preheat the oven to 180°C/350°F/gas mark 4.

Whisk all the ingredients together until thoroughly combined.
Pour into a greased deep 20cm/8-inch pie dish or tin (pan). Cook
for about 45 minutes-1 hour. Serve warm or cold from the dish.

*'Impossible' pies are very popular in the USA. As the mixture cooks, it
forms a crust on the bottom, custard filling in the middle and coconut topping!
Serve it straight from the baking dish.*

Pilgrim pumpkin pie

225g/8 ounces shortcrust (medium-flake) pastry
225g /8 ounces fresh pumpkin purée or 475g/1 pound 1 ounce
  canned pumpkin
2 eggs, beaten
150ml/⅝ cup single (light) cream
75g/3 ounces dark muscovado (soft dark brown) sugar
1 teaspoon ground cinnamon
½ teaspoon ground ginger
Pinch each of grated nutmeg, ground cloves, allspice

Preheat the oven to 190°C/375°F/gas mark 5.

Roll out the dough and line a 23cm/9-inch pie plate. Roll out the
trimmings thinly and cut into leaf shapes. Dampen the edge of
the pie and attach the leaves.

Place all the filling ingredients into a bowl and mix well. Pour into
the pastry case and bake for about 45-50 minutes until the filling
has set. Leave to cool and serve warm with whipped cream or ice
cream.

Pumpkin pie is an essential part of the Thanksgiving celebrations.

Brandy Alexander pie

For the biscuit case
225g/8 ounces digestive biscuits (graham crackers)
50g/½ stick butter, melted
25g/1 ounce sugar

For the filling
115g/1 stick butter
225g/8 ounces golden icing (confectioner's) sugar, sifted
115g/4 ounces plain (dark) chocolate, melted
2 tablespoons brandy
2 tablespoons crème de cacao
150ml/⅝ cup double (heavy) cream
Grated chocolate for sprinkling (optional)

Crush the biscuits (cookies) into fine crumbs and mix with the
melted butter and sugar. Press the mixture onto the base and up
the sides of a shallow 20-23cm/8-9-inch pie or flan dish.

Cream the butter and golden icing sugar until smooth and creamy.
Stir in the melted chocolate, brandy and crème de cacao, mixing
well. Whip the cream until thick but not stiff and fold into the
chocolate mixture.

Spoon into the biscuit crust and chill for several hours before
serving. Sprinkle with grated chocolate just before serving.

The classic ingredients of a Brandy Alexander cocktail – brandy, cream and
crème de cacao (chocolate-flavoured liqueur) are used in this delectably rich,
creamy dessert.

Maple nut pie

225g/8 ounces shortcrust (medium-flake) pastry
200ml/1 cup maple syrup
115g/4 ounces pecans or walnuts, roughly chopped
75g/3 ounces fresh breadcrumbs
3 eggs, beaten
4 tablespoons maple or light muscovado (soft light brown) sugar
Pinch salt
75g/¾ stick butter, melted and cooled

Preheat the oven to 200°C/400°F/gas mark 6.

Roll out the pastry and line a 20-22 cm/8-8½-inch deep flan tin or pie dish. Scatter the nuts over the base, then the breadcrumbs.

Mix together the rest of the ingredients and pour into the pastry case. Bake for 15 minutes, then reduce the oven temperature to 180°C/350°F/gas mark 4 and cook for another 20-25 minutes until the filling is set. Cover with a sheet of foil if the pie is browning too quickly.

Remove from the oven and leave to cool – the filling will sink as the pie cools. Serve warm with whipped cream or ice cream.

Maple syrup is a thin, dark-brown pouring syrup with a distinctive rich, sweet flavour. It is sweeter than sugar and so less is required in cooking. Make sure it says 100-percent maple on the bottle. Real maple syrup is expensive, so if it is really cheap, it probably isn't 100-percent maple. 'Maple flavour' syrup is nothing like the real thing and is best avoided.

Cranberry, orange and pecan pudding

225g/8 ounces cranberries
4 tablespoons fresh orange juice
500ml/2¼ cups milk
200g/7 ounces fresh breadcrumbs
1 egg
75g/3 ounces sugar
1 teaspoon finely grated orange zest
75g/3 ounces walnuts, roughly chopped
Icing (confectioner's) sugar to finish

Soak the cranberries in the orange juice for at least 2 hours.

Heat the milk in a pan and bring to the boil. Remove from the heat and add the breadcrumbs. Stir well and leave until almost cold.

Preheat the oven to 180°C/350°F/gas mark 4. Liberally butter a 23cm/9-inch baking or flan dish.

Beat the breadcrumb and milk mixture until thick, then beat in the egg, most of the sugar, orange zest and half the walnuts. Stir in the soaked cranberries and pour into the dish. Sprinkle with the remaining nuts and sugar.

Bake for 35-45 minutes until golden. Serve hot or cold dredged with sifted icing sugar.

This deliciously moist, fruity pudding has a pleasantly refreshing flavour.

Cranberry fruit cup

2 small tangerines or clementines
2 eating (dessert) apples
Sprig of mint
1 litre/4½ cups cranberry juice
150ml/⅝ cup clementine or orange juice
1 tablespoon lemon juice

Wipe the oranges and apples, then cut them into slices or small dice, removing any pips. Put into a large jug or glass bowl with the mint and add the rest of the ingredients.

Chill very well before serving.

A sophisticated, refreshing cocktail that's ideal for children, drivers and teetotallers.

Winter

CHRISTMAS

The words 'Christes Maesse' appeared in a Saxon book in 1038 and alluded to a religious festival of reflection and quiet prayer to celebrate Christ's birth. But it wasn't until the fourth century that Pope Julius fixed the date as December 25.

Food had an important role in medieval Christmas feasts and was often highly spiced, scented with fragrant rose-water and dyed in glorious, jewelled, stained-glass colours. The yuletide feast began with soup, followed by eggs, fish and meats; then came a roast swan or peacock magnificently arrayed in full plumage, complete with gilded beak and bearing a silver or gold crown. Boar's head was always served at Christmas, glazed with aspic jelly and garlanded with herbs and leaves, its tusks gilded with gold leaf – it must have made an impressive centrepiece. Goose was the chief Christmas bird, and along with other fowl was a popular Christmas gift. Gifts were given throughout the 12 days of Christmas, rather than just on Christmas Day.

Each type of fish, meat and poultry was accompanied by its own particular sauce, and it was the duty of the servers to ensure that the correct sauces were provided in the small dishes placed along the length of the table. *Egerdouce* was a spicy sauce for fish; mustard sauce accompanied boar's head; and pheasant or partridge was served with ginger sauce.

No feast was complete without at least one 'subtlety'. This was an elaborate ornamental table decoration made of sugar paste or marzipan, which portrayed the theme of the feast. The spelling often differed, appearing variously as *soltte*, *solltelle* or *soltette*. They were also known as 'warners', because they were served at the beginning of a banquet to 'warn' (or notify) the guests of the approaching dinner. Christmas themes incorporated angels, shepherds or the Magi. The sugar sculpture, sometimes brightly coloured and festooned with banners, was paraded around the hall so that everyone could admire and marvel at the skill of the cook – and of course, the wealth and generosity of the host. When those present had duly admired and applauded the centrepiece, it was broken up and divided among the diners.

Other traditional foods at this time included frumety (also variously known as *frumety*, *firmity* or *furmentie*) a dish of husked or 'creed' wheat that is probably England's oldest dish. The name is derived from the Latin *frumentum*, meaning 'corn'. Whole wheat was soaked in water, then gently warmed in a low oven for about 12 hours, until the husks swelled and burst. After beating in a mortar, the husks could be rinsed away in a sieve, leaving the now-thick, gelatinous wheat. This jelly was then cooked slowly with milk and thickened with flour or eggs. Frumety was served at the fourteenth-century wedding feast of Henry IV and Joan of Navarre, and also at the coronation of Henry VII. In medieval England it was served as a savoury accompaniment to venison and fish, but gradually became a sweet dish.

A piping-hot bowl of frumety sweetened with honey or treade (molasses) and flavoured with spices and dried fruits was once an essential part of Christmas fare throughout Lancashire and Yorkshire and was often eaten for breakfast on Christmas Day. The taste of frumety has been likened to 'a liquid spice loaf'. Robert Neill, in his novel *Mist Over Pendle,* described the Christmas Eve frumety as '…a great basin of what looked like yellow cream'. A similar dish, made with barley instead of wheat and flavoured with grated nutmeg, was called 'fluffin'.

In east Yorkshire, the arrival of Christmas was heralded by the ringing of the 'frumety bell' in churches in the area at 6 or 7pm on Christmas Eve. This was the signal for housewives to start making the frumety. In the evening, the family gathered in darkness around the fire and set the yule log alight. The yule candle was placed in the centre of the table and was lit by the father or the youngest daughter in the family. A cross was carved in an uncut cheese and everyone wished each other a Merry Christmas and enjoyed bowls of frumenty, followed by cheese and spice cake or apple pie.

In days gone by, northern grocers gave their best customers Christmas gifts of wheat with which to make frumenty. Bakers set aside special days to 'cree', or mill, the wheat, to satisfy the seasonal demand, and their windows displayed artfully arranged pyramids of the cold wheat jelly. Ready-creed or pearled wheat could still be bought in cans as late as the 1930s and was often sweetened with honey, sugar or treacle. At Christmas, expensive luxury foodstuffs such as spices, dried fruits, cream, butter, brandy or rum were often added, too.

Pepys recorded what he ate each Christmas. In 1662, it was 'a mess of brave plum porridge and a roasted pullet': a rather plain meal due to his wife's illness. This was followed by a bought mince pie. On subsequent Christmases he enjoyed richer food, including a 'shoulder of mutton, some good ribs of beef roasted and mince pies'.

By the Elizabethan era, Christmas pie had become an essential part of the festive fare. The origins of the pie date back to the medieval dishes served at the splendid feasts of the wealthy nobility. Spices, sugar and dried fruits imported from the East were very costly, and their use was a flamboyant display of the host's wealth. The idea of cooking meat with dried fruits and spices originated in the Middle East and was brought back by the Crusaders. Hannah Glasse, in her book *The Art of Cookery made Plain and Easy* (1747), gives a recipe for a 'Mutton and Raisin Pie' with a wineglass of rum listed in the ingredients.

In and around the Lake District, the Sunday between Christmas and New Year was the traditional time to make special pies with a filling of minced or chopped mutton, dried fruits, sugar and spices. Jane Grigson, in her book *English Food,* gives a recipe for a 'Sweet Lamb Pie from Westmoreland', which includes candied peel, chopped almonds and orange and lemon juices, among the traditional filling ingredients.

Every region of Britain developed its own Christmas recipes and traditions. Welsh families made taffy (toffee) on Christmas

Eve. Spoonfuls of boiling toffee were dropped into ice-cold water to curl into weird and wonderful shapes.

Scotland's Christmas festivities were banned by the church in 1649 during the Reformation, and most people worked as normal on Christmas Day, so New Year became the more important holiday. In Shetland and Orkney, where there is a deep-seated Norse tradition, Christmas was known by its Norwegian name of *yule* (the ancient feast of the winter solstice) until fairly recently. *Whipkull* or *whipcol*, a mixture of egg yolks beaten with honey or sugar was served in a special bowl to the Shetland *udallers* (lairds), at vast yule breakfasts. Sometimes cream was added, and later still, a good measure of rum or whisky.

In Ireland a few days before Christmas, families went to the Christmas market, or *margadh mór* (literally 'big market') in the nearest town to buy poultry and farm produce. Goose stuffed with mashed potatoes or roast or boiled beef were popular Christmas dishes, while the traditional Christmas Eve meal consisted of fish with creamed potatoes. A large candle was placed in a window and lit to show the Holy Family that there was room and a welcome in that house. The candle was extinguished before the family went to Christmas Mass

The Victorians were largely responsible for making Christmas the joyful festive season it is today. During the nineteenth century, cookery books became enormously popular, and authors like Mrs Beeton (1836-65), in her best-selling *Book of Household Management,* advised readers on all sorts of subjects, including how to create the perfect Christmas dinner.

Cumberland sweet lamb pies

225g/8 ounces lean mutton or lamb, minced (ground)
225g/8 ounces currants
225g/8 ounces raisins
1 cooking apple, peeled and chopped
1 tablespoon candied peel, finely chopped
Juice of 1 lemon
Finely grated zest of ½ lemon
175g/6 ounces light muscovado (soft light brown) sugar
½ teaspoon each of ground mace, cinnamon, pepper and nutmeg
½ teaspoon salt
4 tablespoons dark rum
A little dark beer to mix
350g/12 ounces shortcrust (medium-flake) pastry

Preheat the oven to 180°C/350°F/gas mark 4.

Mix the meat, fruits, lemon juice and zest, sugar, spices and salt until well-combined. Stir in the rum and just enough beer to make a moist mixture.

Roll out half the dough and use to line deep patty or tartlet tins (pans) or a large pie plate or cake tin. Divide the filling among the pastry cases. Roll out the rest of the pastry and cut out lids. Cover the pies and cut 2 slits in each lid. Bake for 20-30 minutes, or until the pastry is golden and the filling cooked through. If making a large pie, you will need to increase the cooking time. Cover the pastry with foil if it becomes too brown.

Cumberland sweet lamb pie is delicious: fruity and spicy rather than sweet and sugary. Apples are added for extra moisture, and the fruits also cut the richness of the mutton or lamb.

Elizabethan-style chicken

175ml/¾ cup robust red wine
3 tablespoons red wine vinegar
50g/2 ounces dried ready-to-eat pears, chopped
115g/4 ounces ready-to-eat prunes, chopped
1 teaspoon ground cinnamon
1 teaspoon ground ginger
Pinch ground cloves
4 x 175g/6 ounce chicken breast fillets
2 tablespoons plain (all-purpose) flour
Salt and pepper
2 tablespoons vegetable oil
175ml/¾ cup chicken stock

Place the wine, wine vinegar, fruits and spices in a shallow dish and add the chicken breasts, spooning the liquid over them. Cover and leave to marinate overnight or for a minimum of 4 hours.

Remove the chicken and dry with kitchen paper (paper towels). Add the salt and pepper to the flour and toss the chicken in this. Heat the oil in a large frying pan or flameproof casserole and fry the chicken on both sides until golden. Remove from the pan.

Drain off the remaining oil and add the chicken stock, reserved marinade and fruit to the pan and bring to the boil. Replace the chicken, cover and simmer for about 30 minutes, or until the chicken is cooked. Put the chicken on a warmed serving plate and boil the remaining liquid in the pan until thickened. Pour over the chicken.

Well-to-do Elizabethans enjoyed sweet, spicy dishes similar to the earlier medieval pottages made with dried fruits, spices and sugar. The Crusaders' experiences in the East greatly influenced English cuisine, and new, exciting foods had been introduced from exotic lands – sugar, almonds, dried fruits, rose-water, citrus fruits and new spices previously unknown in the West such as cloves, nutmeg and mace.

Spiced beef

1 x 2kg /4½ pounds piece silverside (top round) rolled and tied

For the spicing
1 teaspoon sea salt
2 teaspoons black pepper
2 teaspoons English mustard powder
2 teaspoons juniper berries, crushed
55g/2 ounces dark muscovado (soft dark brown) sugar
1 teaspoon each ground allspice, cloves, nutmeg, ginger, ground cinnamon
2 cloves garlic, crushed and chopped finely

For the marinade
150ml/⅝ cup mild olive oil
150ml/⅝ cup red wine
1 tablespoon red wine vinegar

Dry the meat with absorbent kitchen paper (paper towels). Mix together all the spicing ingredients and rub well into the meat. Wrap the meat in greaseproof (waxed) paper and chill for up to 48 hours.

Combine the marinade ingredients. Unwrap the beef and put into a large freezer bag. Pour in the marinade and close the bag securely. Chill for up to 24 hours, turning the bag from time to time to keep the meat covered with the marinade.

Preheat the oven to 220°C/425°F/gas mark 7. Take the meat out of the bag (reserve the marinade) and put into a roasting tin (pan). Cook for 20 minutes, then reduce the temperature to 190°C/375°F/gas mark 5. Allow 20 minutes per 450g/pound for rare, 25 minutes for well-done meat. Spoon over a little of the reserved marinade a couple of times during cooking. When cooked, let the joint stand for 15 minutes before carving. Serve hot or cold.

Molasses and stout glazed ham

1.5-2kg/3-4½ pounds boned and rolled gammon (ham) joint
1 onion quartered
1 stick celery, sliced
5 cloves
2 bay leaves

For the glaze
75g/3 ounces molasses sugar (soft dark brown sugar)
2 tablespoons honey
4 tablespoons stout (or other dark beer)
2 teaspoons English mustard powder

Soak the gammon in cold water for 12-24 hours if needed. (This isn't always necessary; check the directions on the pack). Place in a large pan, cover with cold water and bring to the boil. Skim off any scum. Add the onions, celery, cloves, and bay leaves. Cover and simmer slowly for 1½ hours.

Preheat the oven to 220°C/425°F/gas mark 7.

Place the gammon in a roasting tin (pan); remove the skin, leaving the fat intact. Score the fat into diamond shapes. with a sharp knife. Mix all the ingredients for the glaze together. Spoon over the gammon and cook in the oven for 30-40 minutes, basting 3 or 4 times during cooking. When the fat is golden, transfer to a warm plate and leave for 10 minutes before carving. This is also delicious cold.

A beautifully moist, seasonal favourite packed with flavour. Molasses sugar and stout form a flavoursome, sticky coating.

Sherried potatoes

1 kg/2¼ pounds potatoes
75 g/¾ stick butter
1 tablespoon light muscovado (soft light brown) sugar
½ teaspoon each nutmeg, salt and pepper
1 egg plus 1 egg yolk
3 tablespoons sherry
Finely grated zest and juice of 1 medium orange
1 tablespoon flaked almonds

Peel the potatoes and boil in salted water until tender. Drain and mash the potatoes with the butter, sugar and seasonings.

Preheat the oven to 190°C/375°F/gas mark 5.

Grease a large baking tray. Beat together the egg, egg yolk, sherry, orange zest and juice and beat into the potatoes. Add half the almonds and spoon the mixture into a piping bag. Pipe swirls onto the baking tray. Sprinkle with the remaining almonds and cook for 20-25 minutes, or until browned on top.

These mashed potatoes flavoured with orange juice, sherry and spices add a festive touch and are an excellent accompaniment to roast turkey or goose.

Devilled caviar

(A Bradford Family Recipe)

Thick slices of white bread
Oil for frying
75g/3 ounces caviar
15g/½ ounce butter
Cayenne pepper
Lemon wedges and parsley to garnish

Preheat the oven to 200°C/400°F/gas mark 6. Grease a baking tray.

Using a round 1cm/½-inch cutter, cut out rounds from the bread slices. Scoop out some of the centres to make a hollow. Heat the oil in a frying pan and fry the bread rounds until golden and crisp. Drain on kitchen paper (paper towels).

Spoon a little caviar into the centre of each round. Place a tiny piece of butter on each and sprinkle with cayenne. Put the rounds on the baking tray and bake for 5 minutes. Serve immediately garnished with lemon wedges and parsley.

This dish has been included just for fun, as there is no way that most people can afford to buy caviar these days, let alone adulterate it in this fashion. However, perfectly acceptable substitutes are available; you could try the recipe with one of those as a fun and unusual choice for a drinks-party canapé, and then let people guess whether you have really splashed out or not. RB

Frumenty

115g/4 ounces pearled or kibbled wheat
325ml/1¼ cups creamy milk
25g/1 ounce currants or raisins
1 teaspoon mixed spice
1 teaspoon cinnamon
Honey or sugar to taste

Soak the wheat overnight in a bowl of water, preferably in a warm place.

Drain off the water and place the wheat in a pan with the milk and boil gently for 20 minutes. Add the currants or raisins and simmer gently for another 40 minutes. Beat in the spices and sweeten to taste. Serve hot with cream or a knob of butter and a dash of rum or brandy.

Rich and creamy frumenty makes a nutritious breakfast or pudding.

Iced Christmas pudding

115g/4 ounces mixed dried fruits: raisins, currants, sultanas (white raisins)
50g/2 ounces glacé (candied) cherries, chopped
4 tablespoons rum or brandy
450ml/2¼ cups creamy milk
1 cinnamon stick
3 eggs
115g/4 ounces caster (superfine) sugar
450ml/2 cups whipping cream
1 tablespoon toasted almonds, chopped

Soak the dried fruits and cherries in the rum or brandy overnight.

Pour the milk into a pan and add the cinnamon stick. Heat gently until just about to boil, then remove from the heat, cover and leave for 30 minutes.

Remove the cinnamon stick and reheat the milk over a low heat. Whisk the eggs and sugar together, then pour on the hot milk, whisking all the time. Return the mixture to the pan and heat, stirring, until the custard has thickened, but do not allow to boil. Remove from the heat and leave to cool, stirring occasionally.

Whip the cream until thick but not stiff and fold into the custard with the fruits, soaking liquor and almonds. Pour into a pudding basin, cover and freeze until firm.

Place in the refrigerator for 30 minutes before turning the pudding out onto a serving plate. Decorate with a sprig of holly just before serving.

A cold and creamy alternative for those who find the rich traditional Christmas pudding too heavy after Christmas dinner. Vary the fruits to suit your taste. If you don't like dried fruits, use the same weight of candied fruits.

Christmas compote

600ml/2½ cups fruity red wine
175g/6 ounces light muscovado (soft light brown) sugar
2 sticks cinnamon
4-6 cardamom pods, bruised (optional)
Thick strip of orange zest
Juice of 1 orange
115g/4 ounces kumquats, halved and pips removed
4 tablespoons cranberries
115g/4 ounces ready-to-eat dried apricots
115g/4 ounces ready-to-eat prunes
115g/4 ounces raisins
50g/2 ounces dried figs, halved

Put the wine, sugar, spices and orange zest and juice into a
saucepan and heat gently until the sugar has dissolved. Bring to
the boil and simmer for 10-15 minutes. Add the kumquats and
simmer for 5 minutes, then add the cranberries and simmer for
another 4-5 minutes until the cranberries are soft but still whole.

Using a perforated spoon, transfer the cranberries and kumquats
to a serving bowl, followed by the rest of the fruits. Bring the
spiced-wine mixture to the boil and boil rapidly until reduced by
half. Pour over the fruits, then cool, cover and chill for several
hours. Serve with whipped cream, crème fraîche or ice cream.

*A fragrant, fruity blend of Christmas-pudding flavours – without the
pudding. It can be prepared well ahead of time and stored in the fridge.*

Carol singers' pepper cake

675g/1½ pounds plain (all-purpose) flour
225g/2¼ sticks butter
225g/8 ounces molasses sugar (soft dark brown sugar)
½ teaspoon ground cloves
1 teaspoon ground ginger
1 teaspoon ground cinnamon
½ teaspoon grated nutmeg
675ml/3 cups black treacle (molasses)
4 eggs, beaten
1 teaspoon bicarbonate of soda (baking soda)
4 tablespoons milk

Preheat the oven to 160°C/325°F/gas mark 3. Grease and line a
25 x 35cm/10 x 14-inch roasting tin (pan).

Sift the flour into a mixing bowl and rub in the butter until the
mixture resembles fine breadcrumbs, then add the sugar and
spices. Put the treacle in a small pan and heat gently until melted,
but not hot. Mix into the dry ingredients with the beaten eggs.

Mix the bicarbonate of soda with the milk until dissolved and stir
into the mixture, beating well. Put the mixture into the tin and
bake for 1½-2 hours until cooked through. Cool in the tin, then
turn out onto a wire rack to cool completely.

Store in an airtight tin for a few days before eating, to allow the
flavour to develop.

In Yorkshire, this cake was traditionally given to carol singers at Christmas.
Spicy cakes such as this were known as 'pepper cakes', not because they
contained pepper, but because the spices were imported from the East and the
lands were known collectively as the 'pepper countries'.

Chocolate chestnut log

115g/4 ounces caster sugar
4 eggs
75g/3 ounces plain (all-purpose) flour
25g/1 ounce cocoa powder

For the filling
2 tablespoons brandy
150ml/⅝ cup double (heavy) cream
115g/4 ounces sweetened chestnut purée

For the chocolate butter-cream
75g/3 ounces caster (superfine) sugar
4 tablespoons water
2 egg yolks
115g/1 stick unsalted butter, softened
55g/2 ounces plain (dark) chocolate, melted
Small Christmas decorations

Preheat the oven to 200°C/400°F/gas mark 6. Brush a 23 x 33cm/ 9 x 13-inch Swiss roll tin (pan) with a little oil and line with grease- proof (waxed) paper. Cut a second piece of greaseproof a bit larger than the tin and sprinkle with 2 teaspoons of the sugar. Set aside.

Put the sugar and eggs in a large bowl and whisk until very pale and light, using an electric hand mixer if possible, until the beaters leave a trail on the surface. Sift together the flour and cocoa powder and gently fold into the egg mixture using a metal spoon. Pour into the prepared tin, tilting it so that it covers the whole surface. Bake for 7-9 minutes until firm and springy to the touch.

Turn out the cooked sponge onto the sugared paper. Peel away the lining paper and trim the edges. Cover with a damp tea towel (dishcloth) and cool completely.

Sprinkle the sponge with the brandy. Whip the cream until thick and stir in the chestnut purée. Spread over the sponge and roll up from one long edge.

To make the chocolate butter-cream, heat the sugar and water in a small pan over a low heat until the sugar dissolves. Boil rapidly until syrupy.

Whisk the egg yolks in a bowl and continue whisking while adding the sugar syrup in a steady stream. Whisk until the mixture becomes thick, pale and cool, leaving a trail on the surface. Beat the butter in a separate bowl and gradually beat in the egg mixture until thick and fluffy. Stir in the cooled melted chocolate.

Slice a 7.5cm/3-inch piece from the Swiss roll and cut this small piece in half diagonally. Use a little butter-cream to attach these pieces to the sides of the roll, to represent branches. Cover the log with the rest of the butter-cream and use a skewer or fork to make a bark pattern. Decorate the log with a few small Christmas decorations.

A sophisticated cake flavoured with brandy and filled with a mixture of fresh cream and chestnut purée. You can make the log 2-3 days before Christmas and keep refrigerated. Alternatively, make up in advance, open-freeze then enclose in freezer wrap and store 6-8 weeks. Thaw overnight in the refrigerator.

Snowflake cake

225g/2¼ sticks unsalted butter
225g/8 ounces caster sugar
4 eggs plus 1 egg yolk
75ml/generous ¼ cup fresh orange juice
Finely grated zest 1 orange
225g/8 ounces self-raising (self-rising) flour
1 teaspoon baking powder
115g/4 ounces cranberries
75g/3 ounces almonds, chopped

To finish
100g/3½ ounces apricot jam or preserves
Juice ½ lemon
1 x 450g/1 pound ready-rolled white fondant icing
1 x 500g/1 pound pack royal icing
8 sheets edible rice paper
Silver or gold balls

Preheat the oven to 180°C/350°F/gas mark 4. Grease and line a 20cm/8-inch round cake tin (pan).

Cream the butter and sugar until light and fluffy. Beat in the eggs and yolk, one at a time, followed by the orange juice and zest. Sift in the flour and baking powder and gently fold into the mixture with the cranberries and almonds. Spoon into the prepared tin.

Bake for 50-60 minutes, or until a skewer inserted into the centre comes out clean. Leave to cool in the tin for a few minutes, then finish cooling on a wire rack. This cake keeps well in an airtight tin for up to 5 days.

To decorate, gently warm the apricot jam and lemon juice and brush over the cold cake. Roll out the icing on a surface lightly dusted with icing sugar to a 33cm/13-inch-diameter circle. Using a rolling pin to support the icing, lay it over the cake, smoothing out the top and sides. Trim off any excess and leave to dry for 24 hours.

Make up the royal icing as directed on the package. Draw a snowflake outline about 10cm/4 inches high and 9cm/3½ inches wide on a piece of white paper. Place a sheet of rice paper over the outline and place 2 teaspoons of royal icing in the middle. Use a small brush to fill in the outline. Repeat with the remaining sheets of rice paper and royal icing. Press the sliver balls into the snowflakes and leave to dry for 24 hours.

Cut out the snowflakes, leaving the rice paper attached to the back and stick onto the cake using a little royal icing or apricot jam to secure. Leave to dry for about 3 hours before serving.

A light, fruity Christmas cake made using ready-rolled fondant icing and a packet of royal icing for speed.

Rum or brandy butter tarts

225g/8 ounces shortcrust (medium-flake) pastry
150g/5½ ounces dried fruits, chopped
2 tablespoons rum or brandy
55g/2 ounces rum or brandy butter
55g/2 ounces dark muscovado (soft dark brown) sugar
1 egg, beaten
25g/1 ounce ground almonds
½ teaspoon ground cinnamon
Icing (confectioner's) sugar for dusting

Preheat the oven to 190°C/375°F/gas mark 5.

Roll out the pastry on a floured surface and cut out 12-15 rounds using a 7.5cm/3-inch fluted cutter. Line a bun tin (patty or tart pan) with the pastry rounds.

Mix the dried fruits with the rum or brandy and leave for 10 minutes. Cream the rum butter with the muscovado sugar until light, then beat in the egg, ground almonds and cinnamon, followed by the soaked fruit. Place a dessertspoonful of filling into each pastry case and bake for 15-20 minutes.

Cool in the tins for a few minutes, then place on a wire tray to cool. Serve warm or cold dusted with icing sugar.

Use whatever dried fruits you have to hand – dates, sultanas (white raisins), apricots, etc. (or you can use mincemeat instead) to make these scrumptious little tarts.

Russet apple mincemeat

225g/8 ounces shredded suet
225g/8 ounces dried apricots, chopped
225g/8 ounces cooking apples, peeled, cored and chopped
225g/8 ounces prunes, chopped
225g/8 ounces sultanas (white raisins)
115g/4 ounces glacé (candied) cherries, chopped
115g/4 ounces candied peel, finely diced
55g/2 ounces almonds, chopped
1 tablespoon honey
1 teaspoon ground cinnamon
Large pinch of ground cloves
Finely grated zest and juice of 1 lemon
Finely grated zest and juice of 1 orange
600ml/2½ cups ginger wine

Combine all the ingredients in a large mixing bowl, stirring very
well. Cover and leave to stand overnight to allow the flavours to
blend. Pack into cold, sterilized jars, making sure there are no air
bubbles and cover with waxed discs, then with tight-fitting plastic
or metal lids.

*An old country recipe for an unusual but delectable mincemeat. Mincemeat
was first recorded in the sixteenth century and contained minced or shredded
meat, dried fruits and spices and, by the seventeenth century, alcohol.
Mincemeat will keep for a year in a dry cool place as long as enough alcohol
is added to preserve the ingredients.*

Mincemeat pudding

75g/¾ stick butter
75g/3 ounces dark muscovado (soft dark brown) sugar
2 eggs, beaten
115g/4 ounces self-raising (self-rising) flour
225g/8 ounces mincemeat

Preheat the oven to 170°C/350°F/gas mark 3. Butter a shallow 20cm/8-inch baking dish.

Cream the butter and sugar until light. Gradually beat in the eggs. Gently fold in the flour, followed by the mincemeat. Spoon into the dish and cook for 10 minutes, then reduce the heat to 160°C/325°F/gas mark 3 and cook for about another 30 minutes until cooked through and golden.

Serve with cream or custard.

A quick-and-easy winter pudding for when time is short.

Mince pie parcels

225g/8 ounces plain (all-purpose) flour
4 egg yolks
50g/2 ounces caster (superfine) sugar
115g/1 stick butter
350g/12 ounces mincemeat
Egg white to glaze
Caster sugar for sprinkling

Sift the flour into a mixing bowl and make a well in the centre. Put the egg yolks, sugar and butter into the well and work with your hands until everything is well combined, gradually drawing in the flour. Knead lightly until smooth. Wrap in cling film (plastic wrap) and chill for 1 hour.

Divide the dough in half. Roll each piece into a rectangle about 30 x 23cm/12 x 9 inches on a floured surface. Spoon 12-24 spoonfuls of mincemeat evenly in lines across one piece of dough. Dampen between the mincemeat and the edges and cover with the other half of the dough. Press the dough between the mincemeat to seal. Cut into squares with a pastry wheel or a knife and place on baking trays. Knead and re-roll the pastry trimmings to make more parcels. Chill for 20 minutes.

Preheat the oven to 200°C/400°F/gas mark 6. Bake for 10 minutes. Brush with beaten egg white and sprinkle with sugar. Return to the oven for another 5 minutes until browned. Cool on a wire rack, then store in an airtight container.

These are much quicker to make than ordinary mince pies and you can make them any size.

Chocolate rum truffles

115g/4 ounces plain or milk chocolate (at least 60% cocoa solids), chopped
75g/3 ounces cake crumbs
75g/3 ounces golden icing (confectioner's) sugar, sifted
75g/3 ounces ground almonds or hazelnuts
2 tablespoons dark rum
4 tablespoons double (heavy) cream
55g sifted cocoa powder, chopped nuts or chocolate
  vermicelli, to coat

Melt the chocolate in a bowl over a pan of hot,
not boiling, water.

In a large bowl, mix the crumbs, sugar, ground almonds and rum
until combined, and then gradually add the melted chocolate,
mixing well. Stir in the cream. Chill the mixture in the refrigerator
for at least 1 hour until firm enough to handle.

Take teaspoons of the chilled mixture and roll into balls; you
should get about 30. Roll the balls in the coating of your choice.
These will keep in the refrigerator for up to 2 weeks.

*These delectable little morsels are traditionally eaten at Christmas. They first
appeared named as 'truffles' in the Army and Navy Store's catalogue of 1926.*
  *The possibilities for chocolate truffles are infinite. Substitute the rum with
orange juice, whisky, brandy or liqueur; use white chocolate; roll them in
coconut or golden icing sugar… whatever you like best!*

NEW YEAR

More than the people of any other nation, the Scots are renowned for celebrating the start of the New Year, which in Scotland is called Hogmanay. The origins of the word 'Hogmanay' are unknown, although it may derive from the Norse *hoggunott*, or 'night of slaughter', when animals were killed for a midwinter feast, or possibly from *aguillanneuf* the old French street cry for gifts on New Year's Eve.

'First footing' – visiting friends and relatives immediately after New Year's Eve, in the early hours of the morning of January 1 and after the bells have rung in the New Year – is still common. Tradition dictates that the 'first foot' in the house after midnight should be male, dark and handsome and should carry symbolic coal, shortbread, salt, black bun and, of course, whisky. Shortbread and black bun were reserved for 'high days and holidays', and were luxurious delicacies for the majority of people because only the wealthy could afford the costly ingredients. Every region of Scotland created its own particular shortbread, such as Yetholm bannock, which incorporates finely chopped stem ginger.

Scotland's national biscuit (cookie), shortbread is sold throughout the world and is recognized for its superb 'short', crumbly, melt-in-the-mouth texture and rich, buttery flavour. It is thought that the custom of eating shortbread at New Year originated in the ancient pagan yule cakes, which symbolized the sun.

Black bun, a rich, dark, heavily fruited cake, is distinguished by being encased in pastry. Originally the purpose of the pastry was to protect the outside of the cake from burning during cooking and to help keep the cake in shape. After cooking, the fruit-soaked pastry was discarded and given to servants and beggars. Today, the pastry is richer and is an integral part of the cake.

Cloutie dumpling ('cloutie' is the cloth in which the pudding is boiled), a fruit pudding that is less rich than English Christmas pudding, is traditionally served at Hogmanay. On New Year's Day any leftovers are fried for breakfast with bacon and eggs.

Until well into the nineteenth century, the traditional Hogmanay beverage was 'het pint': a heady blend of hot spiced ale, eggs and whisky. A couple of hours before midnight, large copper kettles of het pint were hawked around the streets. The carriers of the kettles were accompanied by cupbearers, who urged passers-by enjoy a 'noggin' from the steaming kettles.

In Kirkwall, Orkney, a 'New Year ba' game' takes place in the streets of the town on January 1, between the 'Uppies' and 'Doonies', (Up-the-Gates and Doon-the-Gates) from Old Norse *gata* 'path' or 'road'.

The traditional New Year song is 'Auld Lang Syne', although the original author remains unknown and the version sung today was reworked by Robert Burns.

Long ago throughout the British Isles, yule logs were blessed with wine by the parish priest, and even the farm animals found ale or spirits mixed in with their New Year feed. Priests also blessed wine and beer, and strong church ales were sold in churchyards to welcome in the coming year. The custom has survived to the present day, when glasses are filled as midnight strikes and a toast is drunk for health and happiness in the year ahead.

Highland shortbread

225g/8 ounces plain (all-purpose) flour
115g/4 ounces rice flour
115g/4 ounces icing (confectioner's) sugar
225g/2¼ sticks unsalted butter
Caster (superfine) sugar for sprinkling

Preheat the oven to 150°C/300°F/gas mark 2.

Lightly grease a large baking tray. Sift the flours and icing sugar into a mixing bowl. Knead in the butter and mix to a soft dough. Pat the dough out into 4 rounds about 1cm/½-inch thick. Prick the top and flute the edges with finger and thumb.

Place the rounds on the baking tray and bake for about 40 minutes until cooked but still pale. Sprinkle with caster sugar and store in an airtight tin.

When making shortbread, ground rice or rice flour sometimes replaces some of the flour in a recipe. This gives the shortbread a fine, crunchy texture. Only butter should be used. The more butter the shortbread contains, the 'shorter' and crumblier the shortbread. Don't roll out the dough, or it will become tough. Shortbread must not be allowed to brown during cooking, but should remain pale.

Black bun

75g/¾ stick butter
350g/12 ounces plain (all-purpose) flour
pinch of salt
2 tablespoons sugar
2 eggs, beaten
Iced water to mix
350g/12 ounces raisins
350g/12 ounces currants
225g/8 ounces blanched almonds, chopped
115g/4 ounces mixed peel, chopped
225g/8 ounces plain (all-purpose) flour
1½ teaspoons baking powder
1 teaspoon ground mixed spice
½ teaspoon ground ginger
½ teaspoon ground cinnamon
Generous pinch of ground mace
115g/4 ounces dark muscovado (soft dark brown) sugar
2 tablespoons whisky
1 egg, beaten
175ml/¾ cup milk

Grease an 18cm/7-inch round cake tin (pan).

Rub the butter into the flour until the mixture resembles bread-crumbs. Stir in the salt and sugar, followed by the eggs. Mix well, adding enough iced water to make a stiff dough. Knead gently on a floured surface, wrap in cling film (plastic wrap) and chill for at least 30 minutes.

Divide the dough in two, with one piece slightly larger than the other. Roll out the larger piece of dough into a circle large enough to fit the base and sides of the tin. Ease the pastry into the cake tin, pressing into the base and sides. Trim off any excess dough and put the tin in the fridge to chill.

Preheat the oven to 170°C/350°F/gas mark 3.

Mix the raisins, currants, almonds and peel. Sift in the flour, baking powder and spices and stir in the sugar. Add the whisky, egg and enough milk to bind the mixture together and mix well. Spoon the filling into the lined tin and press flat.

Roll out the smaller piece of dough in a circle to cover the mixture. Dampen the edges of the dough with water and lay over the filling. Press the edges together to seal. Trim any excess dough and lightly prick the surface with a fork. Brush with beaten egg to glaze. Bake for 2½ to 3 hours, testing with a skewer inserted into the centre of the cake which should come out clean; if not, continue cooking.

Cool in the tin and then turn onto a wire rack. Allow to become cold before storing in an airtight tin. Make this 2-3 weeks before you plan to eat it, to allow the flavours to mature.

Dried fruits have been enjoyed since antiquity, when fresh fruits such as figs and dates were laid out in the hot sun to dry. Among the most popular dried fruits in Britain are currants, raisins and sultanas (white raisins), which all come from different types of grapes. In the Middle Ages, currants were known as 'raisins of Corinth', due to the fact that they were imported from Corinth in Greece.

Raisins, too, were imported from Mediterranean countries; Muscatel raisins, although more expensive, are the finest: plump and full of rich, sweet flavour. Sultanas (white raisins), paler than currants and regular raisins, are dried white grapes and originally came from Smyrna (now Izmir) in Turkey but are now produced in several hot countries around the world.

Vegetable croustades

75g/¾ stick butter
24 slices bread (white or brown)
2 tablespoons olive oil
1 pepper, seeds removed and diced
1-2 cloves garlic, crushed
1 onion, finely chopped
1 small aubergine (eggplant), peeled and diced
225g/8 ounces ripe tomatoes, skinned, seeds removed and chopped
1 tablespoon finely chopped thyme
Salt and pepper

Preheat the oven to 200°C/400°F/gas mark 6.

Melt the butter and use some to brush 24 patty tins (pans). Using a 3.5cm/1½ inch biscuit (cookie) cutter, cut a circle from each slice of bread and flatten with a rolling pin. Press the rounds into the patty tins and brush with the remaining melted butter. Bake for 15-20 minutes until crisp and golden.

Heat the oil in a pan and cook the pepper, garlic and onion for about 3 minutes over a high heat. Add the aubergine (eggplant) and cook for another 2 minutes until soft, then add the tomatoes, herbs and seasoning and cook for 2 minutes, stirring all the time. Season with salt and pepper, cover and simmer for 15 minutes until thickened. Spoon into the baked croustades and serve.

Tasty croustades made from sliced bread are perfect for a New Year's Eve party. Once filled, they'll stay crisp for 2-3 hours.

Mini baked potatoes with Calvados chicken

900g/2 pounds small new potatoes
2 tablespoons oil
Sea salt
55g/½ stick butter
3 skinless, boneless chicken breasts, sliced
2 tablespoons Calvados or cider (applejack)
50g/2 ounces apple purée or apple sauce
Salt and pepper

Preheat the oven to 200°C/400°F/gas mark 6.

Scrub and dry the potatoes and rub with oil to coat. Place in a roasting tin (pan) and sprinkle with sea salt. Bake for about 50 minutes, depending on size.

Meanwhile, melt the butter in a frying pan and add the chicken breasts. Cook until the chicken is cooked through, then add the Calvados, apple sauce and seasoning to taste. Put the mixture in a food processor or blender and work to a smooth paste.

Put the mixture into a piping bag with a small plain nozzle. Make a slit in each potato and pipe the chicken mixture into each. Place on a lightly greased baking tray and heat through in the oven before serving.

These tiny baked potatoes filled with a scrumptious savoury filling are ideal for a buffet party.

Smoked salmon parcels with cream cheese

15 slices smoked salmon
175g/6 ounces cream cheese, softened
Salt and black pepper

Cut the salmon slices in half and place some cream cheese at the end of each slice. Season well with a little salt and plenty of black pepper. Roll up each slice and secure with a cocktail stick if you wish.

Serve on a large serving platter garnished with crisp, green salad leaves.

Smoked salmon and cream cheese is a flavoursome combination for a party.

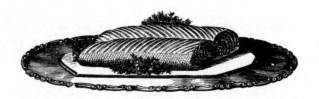

Cloutie dumpling

225g/8 ounces self-raising (self-rising) flour
1 teaspoon each of ground cinnamon, mixed spice, ginger
225g/8 ounces light muscovado (soft light brown) sugar
115g/4 ounces shredded suet (or shortening)
225g/8 ounces currants/sultanas (white raisins), mixed
225ml/1 cup milk and whisky, mixed in any proportions

Sift the flour and spices into a mixing bowl. Add the sugar, suet and
dried fruit and mix to a soft consistency with the milk and whisky.

Wring out a large square of cotton cloth in boiling water. Spread
the cloth out and sprinkle generously with flour. Put the pudding
mixture in the centre, gather up the ends of the cloth and tie
tightly with string – leaving room for the pudding to expand
during cooking. Alternatively, put the mixture into a greased
1½ litre/1½-quart pudding basin, place an upturned plate in the
bottom of a large pan, set the pudding on top of the plate and
pour in boiling water to come about ¼ of the way up the pudding.
Bring to simmering point and simmer steadily for 3 hours, topping
up with boiling water as necessary.

Dip the pudding in cold water (this stops the 'skin' sticking to the
cloth) and untie the cloth. Place on a large plate and dry off in a
low oven.

Serve with spiced whisky cream sauce (see page 260) or custard.
It's also delicious with rum and raisin ice cream (see page 262).

This delightful pudding is traditionally served at Hogmanay (New Year).
Coins wrapped in greaseproof (waxed) paper are stirred into the mixture
before cooking.

Spiced whisky cream sauce

600ml / 2½ cups double (heavy) or whipping cream
4 teaspoons ground ginger
4 teaspoons ground cinnamon
½ teaspoon grated nutmeg
4 tablespoons light muscovado (soft light brown) sugar
2-4 tablespoons whisky (single malt or blended)

Heat the cream, spices and sugar in a non-stick pan over a low heat until the sugar has dissolved completely.

Bring to the boil and simmer for about 3 minutes, stirring.

Remove from the heat and add the whisky. Serve hot with cloutie dumpling (see page 259).

This rich, creamy sauce is enhanced with Scotch whisky and is just as delicious with other hot steamed puddings.

Rum and raisin ice cream

175g/6 ounces raisins
4 tablespoons rum
450ml/2 cups creamy milk
1 cinnamon stick, broken
3 eggs
115g/4 ounces demerara (light brown cane) sugar
450ml/2 cups whipping cream

Soak the raisins in the rum overnight.

Heat the milk in a pan with the pieces of cinnamon stick until almost boiling. Remove from the heat, cover and leave for 45 minutes, then remove the cinnamon pieces.

Whisk the eggs and sugar until blended. Heat the milk again to just below boiling point and pour onto the egg mixture, whisking all the time. Return to the pan and cook over a low heat, stirring until the mixture thickens, but do not allow to boil. Remove from the heat and leave to cool, stirring occasionally.

Whisk the cream until thick, then fold into the custard with the fruit and any soaking liquor. Pour into a freezer-proof container and cover and freeze until firm. Place in the refrigerator 30 minutes before serving.

You can use other dried fruits instead of the raisins, e.g. sultanas (white raisins), currants, candied peel or a mixture. If you have no rum to hand, substitute brandy or whisky instead.

Iced fruit bombe

115g/4 ounces mixed dried blueberries and cranberries
50g/2 ounces glacé (candied) cherries
50g/2 ounces dried mango, chopped
50g/2 ounces candied cantaloupe or glacé cherries
4 tablespoons fruit liqueur, e.g. orange
4 eggs, separated
115g/4 ounces icing (confectioner's) sugar
300ml/1¼ cups double (heavy) cream, whipped
50g/2 ounces flaked almonds or chopped hazelnuts

Soak the fruits in the liqueur in a covered bowl overnight.
Next day, whisk the egg yolks and sugar until thick and light. In a separate bowl whisk the egg whites until stiff but not dry, then fold into the egg yolks with the whipped cream.

Pour into a freezer-proof container and freeze until just firm around the edges. Remove from the freezer and stir in the soaked fruits, liqueur and nuts. Spoon into a 1.1-litre/1-quart pudding basin, then cover and freeze until firm.

Turn out onto a serving plate about 20 minutes before serving and keep in the refrigerator until needed.

This lusciously creamy, chilled ice cream studded with colourful candied fruits makes a sumptuous New Year's dessert.

Chocolate rum truffle gateau

450g/1 pound plain (dark) chocolate (minimum 70% cocoa solids), chopped
4 tablespoons dark rum
5 tablespoons golden syrup (corn syrup)
600ml/2½ cups double (heavy) cream
Cocoa powder to finish

Brush a 25cm/10-inch loose-based or springform round cake tin with oil and line the base with non-stick baking parchment.

Put the chocolate, rum and golden syrup (corn syrup) in a heatproof bowl over a pan of simmering (not boiling) water and stir until melted. Remove the bowl and allow to cool slightly.

Whisk the cream lightly until it just holds its shape and fold one-third into the chocolate mixture. Fold in the rest of the cream and pour into the prepared tin. Tap the tin to release any air bubbles and cover with cling film (plastic wrap). Chill for several hours or overnight.

Remove from the tin, place on a serving plate and dredge with sieved cocoa powder.

A very rich and impressive chocolate dessert that's perfect for New Year celebrations.

Port wine jellies

150g/5½ ounces caster (superfine) sugar
425ml/1⅞ cups cold water
Thinly pared rind and juice of 1 lemon
3 tablespoons powdered gelatine
600ml/2½ cups port
Whipped cream to decorate

Put 75g/3 ounces of the sugar in a pan together with the water and the lemon rind and juice. Cover and bring to the boil, then remove from the heat and cool slightly. Sprinkle over the gelatine, whisking until dissolved. Leave to stand for about 10 minutes, whisking occasionally, until the gelatine has dissolved completely.

Strain the syrup into a bowl and discard the lemon rind. Stir in the wine and add more sugar to taste; the mixture should be stronger and sweeter than usual as this will lessen as the mixture chills.

Pour into 8 stemmed glasses and chill until set. Top with whipped cream to serve.

The deep-ruby colour of this refreshing sweet looks stunning when topped with whipped cream.

Liqueur frosted almonds

¾ cup sugar*
¼ cup liqueur, e.g. amaretto
1½ cups whole almonds

Put the sugar and liqueur into a heavy-based pan and heat gently until the sugar has dissolved. Increase the heat and boil for 6 minutes, brushing down the sides of the pan with a pastry brush dipped in water while the mixture is cooking; this prevents the sugar from crystallizing on the sides of the pan.

Remove from the heat and stir in the nuts. Keep stirring until the mixture becomes cloudy, then tip onto a non-stick baking tray or baking tray lined with non-stick baking paper. Leave to cool for 15-20 minutes, then break into pieces. When completely cold, store in an airtight tin for up to a week.

It doesn't matter what size cup you use, as long as the proportions are correct.

You can use any liqueur left over from Christmas – Cointreau, etc. – or try walnut liqueur with walnuts or Frangelico with hazelnuts.

Whisky punch

1 *large orange*
2 *lemons*
225g/8 *ounces light muscovado (soft light brown) sugar*
3-5 *cloves*
2 *cinnamon sticks*
1 *litre/4½ cups boiling water*
1 *bottle whisky*
150ml/⅝ *cup ginger wine*

Slice the fruit into a large serving bowl. Combine the sugar, spices and boiling water and pour over the fruit. Allow to cool.

Add the whisky and ginger wine, cover and leave to stand for at least 4 hours.

Reheat gently (don't allow it to boil) and serve in heatproof glasses.

A wonderfully warming New Year's Eve drink.

Het pint

1.2 litres/5 cups pale ale
1 teaspoon grated nutmeg
Sugar to taste
300ml/1¼ cups whisky

Heat the ale and nutmeg in a large pan until very hot, but don't
allow to boil. Stir in the sugar to taste, then add the whisky and
heat gently.

Pour into a heatproof bowl or heatproof glasses and serve hot.

This modern recipe omits the eggs which were used in the original recipe.

TWELFTH NIGHT

Christmas in medieval England, Scotland and Wales was an immensely popular 12-day festival, with the celebrations reaching their peak in a spectacular finale on January 6, or Twelfth Night: the Feast of the Epiphany. It was also the custom to appoint a boy bishop to take the place of his senior chaplain at Windsor. The festivities included feasting, dancing, singing and general merriment and were presided over by the 'Lord of Misrule', who was accompanied by his retinue of costumed entertainers, acrobats, fools and jesters.

Medieval monarchs wore their finest regalia, and gifts were given throughout the 12 days of Christmas to commemorate the gifts given by the Three Kings to the baby Jesus. In the Chapel Royal in St James's Palace, London, an Epiphany service was held annually for 900 years to commemorate the gifts of the Magi to the infant Jesus. Afterwards a gift of money was given to charity, frankincense to a church and myrrh to a hospital.

A sumptuous banquet marked Twelfth Night, and included a lavishly spiced fruit cake and a large savoury pie, which had pride of place on the table. Wassail, the drink of good wishes, has been associated with Twelfth Night since the 1400s. The choir of the Chapel Royal sang as the wassail cup, which contained spiced ale sweetened with honey, was brought in by the Lord Steward and presented to the King and Queen, and then passed around the table. These bowls were often made of silver or pewter and were elaborate, ornate and many-handled. 'Wassail' comes from the Old English term *waes hael,* meaning 'be well' or 'good health'.

Farmers used to wassail their orchards and fields on January 6 to ensure a plentiful and successful harvest. Wassail still survives in West Country apple orchards: cider is poured around the roots of the best tree, guns are fired through the branches and a piece of toast is placed in the branches while everyone sings the 'wassail song', asking the trees to bear large crops of juicy fruit. As the wassail bowl is passed around, the drinkers make a wish for a successful year's farming and a bumper crop at harvest time.

Twelfth Night pie contained a selection of meats and dried fruits and 'joke' pies were also made. When one of these pies was cut open, a flock of live birds flew out – to the astonishment and delight of the guests. This was the source of the nursery-rhyme reference to the 'four and twenty blackbirds baked in a pie', which began to sing when the pie was opened.

Twelfth Night cake dates back to the fourteenth century and wasn't iced, but instead was decorated with colourful candied fruits and contained a bean and a pea. The man who found the bean in his slice became king of the festivities for the evening and the woman who found the pea was queen. In 1563, Mary Queen of Scots was present at the cutting of the Twelfth Night cake at Holyrood Palace, when her maid, Mary Fleming, discovered the pea, and was dressed in her royal mistress's robes for the remainder of the day. In later years charms with symbolic meanings were also hidden in the cake.

Twelfth Night cakes became increasingly large and showy. London pastry cooks displayed cakes of every shape, size and price in their windows. Decorations were sold separately and included stars, castles, kings, churches and many others besides and could be pure white or painted with edible colourings. In 1811, the following announcement appeared:

> *Extraordinary Large Twelfth Night Cake, 18 feet in circumference, to be seen at Adam's, 41 Cheapside … The cake considerably surpasses in size any that had been made in London, or, in fact, the world: its weight is nearly half a ton, and actually contains nearly two hundred and a half weight of currants and upwards of one thousand eggs…*

In Glamorganshire in Wales, an enormous loaf or cake was prepared, which was then divided into three parts to represent Christ, the Virgin Mary and the Three Kings. Rings were hidden in the cake, and whoever found a ring in his or her slice was elected as King or Queen of Misrule and presided over the day's festivities.

Twelfth Night continued to be celebrated in great style with grand parties until the Reformation. Samuel Pepys noted in his diary that he hosted an event on Twelfth Night, with masques, plays, dancing, singing, gambling and other revelries.

After the Reformation, Twelfth Night celebrations were banned by the Puritans, and fell into disuse, although they were gradually revived but without the earlier religious overtones. By 1870, Twelfth Night had become a time of mischief and over-indulgence. Queen Victoria announced that she felt it was unseemly to hold such an irreligious festival, and Twelfth Night was banned as a feast day. The confectioners who made Twelfth Night cakes were left with redundant figurines and models for the cakes, and lost revenue by the banning of the feast. As a result, they began to decorate the cakes with snowy scenes and sold them for Christmas instead. This was the beginning of the modern Christmas cake, the direct descendant of Twelfth Night cake.

In the Green Room of London's Drury Lane Theatre, however, Twelfth Night cake is still eaten and a toast drunk in honour of Richard Baddeley, a pastry cook who later became an actor. When he died in 1794, he bequeathed the sum of £100, invested at three percent interest, to provide a cake, known as the 'Baddeley Cake', which was to be eaten annually, in his memory by the cast performing at the theatre. The ancient ceremony, interrupted only by war, was revived in 1947.

Twelfth Night game pie

<u>*For the filling*</u>
450g/1 pound game meat, e.g. grouse, pheasant or partridge
125ml/generous ½ cup fortified red wine (e.g. port or Madeira)
115g/4 ounces raisins
115g/4 ounces ready-to-eat prunes, chopped
Salt and pepper
350g/12 ounces lean pork
225g/8 ounces rashers of bacon, lean and fat
½ teaspoon each grated nutmeg, ginger,
  and cinnamon
Pinch of ground cloves
300ml/1¼ cups game or meat stock

<u>*For the pastry*</u>
450g/1 pound plain (all-purpose) flour
1 teaspoon salt
175ml/¾ cup water (approx.)
225g/8 ounces lard
1 egg yolk
1 beaten egg to glaze
1 egg yolk beaten with a good pinch of saffron to glaze

Slice the game into thin slices approximately 5cm/2 inches in length, reserving any trimmings. Marinate in the wine with the dried fruits and salt and pepper for a few hours.

Roughly chop the game trimmings (or use a food processor), pork and bacon, stir in the spices and season well with salt and pepper.

To make the pastry, sift the flour and salt into a mixing bowl and make a well in the centre. Place the water and lard in a saucepan and bring to the boil. Pour immediately into the well, stirring vigorously (or use an electric mixer) then add the egg yolk, beating well.

Turn out onto a floured board. As soon as it is comfortable to handle, knead until pliable and soft. Do not allow the pastry to cool too much and do not use while still very hot, or the dough will collapse during shaping. It should be pleasantly warm.

Roll out two-thirds of the dough (wrap the remainder in cling film/plastic wrap in a warm place) about 6mm/¼-inch thick and ease quickly into the base and up the sides of a hinged mould or an 18cm/7-inch loose-based cake tin (pan).

Preheat the oven to 230°C/450°F/gas mark 8. Pat dry the game. Place half the pork and bacon mixture in the base of the pastry-lined mould and spoon over half the marinated fruits. Cover with the sliced game and top with the remaining fruits. Cover with the rest of the pork mixture.

Roll out the remaining dough and gently place on top of the pie. Press on firmly and trim any excess with a sharp knife. Decorate the edge and seal well. Make a central hole in the pie and decorate with pastry leaves, roses, etc., using a little of the beaten egg glaze to stick them. Glaze the exposed pastry with beaten egg and place on a baking tray. Bake for 20 minutes, then reduce the temperature to 160°C/325°F/gas mark 3, cover the pie with foil and bake for a further 3 hours.

Remove the pie from the oven, cool slightly and remove from the mould or tin. Brush all over with the egg yolk and saffron mixture and return to the oven until the glaze is set. Remove from the oven and allow to cool.

When the pie is almost cold, pour into it as much of the cool stock as it will take, pouring slowly through a small funnel. Leave for several hours in a cool place before serving, by which time the stock will have set to a jelly.

This is a good way of using older, tougher game meat. If you are artistic and used to handling hot-water-crust pastry, the dough can be moulded by hand into a crenellated or turreted pie.

Pheasant breast fillets with spiced red cabbage

1 medium red cabbage
2 large onions, chopped
2 cooking apples, peeled, cored and chopped
1 garlic clove, crushed
½ teaspoon grated nutmeg
¼ teaspoon ground cloves
1 tablespoon juniper berries, crushed
3 tablespoons dark muscovado (soft dark brown) sugar
3 tablespoons red wine vinegar
1 tablespoon lemon juice
25g/¼ stick butter
4 pheasant breast fillets
Salt and pepper
50g/½ stick butter

Preheat the oven to 150°C/300°F/gas mark. Grease a large baking dish or casserole. Shred the cabbage leaves finely (you can do this in a food processor). Layer the cabbage, onions and apples in a greased ovenproof dish or casserole, sprinkling each layer with the garlic, spices and sugar. Mix the wine vinegar with the lemon juice and pour over the contents of the dish. Dot with the butter and cover tightly. Cook for 2-2½ hours, stirring once during the cooking time.

Lightly season the pheasant fillets with the salt and pepper. Melt the butter in a frying pan over a medium to high heat; when it sizzles, put the fillets in the pan and quickly brown all over. Reduce the heat and cook gently for a further 15-20 minutes. It is cooked when the juices run clear and there is no pink meat. Arrange the red cabbage on a plate and place the fillets on top to serve.

Pheasant has a milder flavour than grouse. After hanging (depending on age and the weather), the flesh develops a mild, gamy flavour.

Venison steaks with red wine

6 x 175g/6-ounce venison steaks
1 onion, finely chopped
1 bay leaf
1 sprig thyme
6 juniper berries, lightly crushed
300ml/1¼ cups full-bodied red wine
25g/¼ stick butter
1 tablespoon oil
2 tablespoons redcurrant jelly
Salt and pepper

Put the steaks in a large shallow dish and sprinkle with the onion, herbs and juniper berries. Pour over the wine, cover and marinate in the refrigerator for at least 4 hours or overnight, turning the steaks from time to time.

Remove the steaks from the marinade (reserve the marinade) and dry with absorbent kitchen paper (paper towels). Heat the butter and oil in a frying pan and fry the steaks for 4 minutes on each side. Keep warm while you make the sauce.

Strain the marinade into the frying pan and stir to loosen any sediment on the bottom of the pan. Bring to the boil and boil rapidly for a few minutes until the liquid has reduced. Stir in the redcurrant jelly and season to taste. Cook for another 2 minutes stirring, then pour over the steaks and serve immediately.

Strong-flavoured venison needs to be matched with robust flavours such as red wine and spices. Farmed venison is not as strong-tasting and has a less 'gamy' flavour than wild, but the animal's age and length of hanging time will greatly influence the meat's flavour and texture. Some deer are hung for a few days, others for a fortnight, by which time they develop a 'high', strong flavour.

Braised celery

(Bradford Family Recipe)

2 heads of celery, trimmed and cut into short lengths
25g/¼ stick butter
1 onion, chopped
1 carrot, chopped
1 slice of bacon, diced
300ml/1¼ cups stock
Salt and pepper

Preheat the oven to 190°C/375°F/gas mark 5. Grease a baking dish.

Put the celery pieces into a pan and just cover with water. Add a pinch of salt and bring to the boil. Boil for 1 minute, remove from the heat and drain well.

Heat the butter in a frying pan and gently cook the onion, carrot and bacon until soft. Place the celery in the baking dish with the vegetables and bacon, cover and bake for 20 minutes. Pour in the stock and season with salt and pepper. Continue cooking until the celery is tender.

Braised celery: you either love it or hate it. In my case and my late father's it was the latter, as I cannot abide it in almost any form. However, this dish is tasty enough to render it palatable, even to me, and therefore should be a resounding success with those who really like it. RB

Twelfth Night cake

500g/1⅛ pounds sultanas (white raisins)
250g/9 ounces candied peel, chopped
250g/9 ounces raisins
250g/9 ounces prunes, chopped
115g/4 ounces currants
100g/3½ ounces glacé (candied) cherries, quartered
100ml/scant ½ cup orange juice
250ml/1⅛ cups orange liqueur
250g/2½ sticks butter
115g/4 ounces dark muscovado (soft dark brown) sugar
5 eggs
Grated zest of ½ orange
250g/9 ounces plain (all-purpose) flour
60g/2¼ ounces almonds, chopped

Place the fruits in a large bowl and pour over the orange juice and liqueur. Cover tightly and leave for 2-3 days until the fruit has absorbed the liquid.

Preheat the oven to 150°C/300°F/gas mark 2. Grease a 23cm/9-inch round deep cake tin (pan) and line with a double thickness of greaseproof (waxed) paper. Lightly grease the paper.

Beat the butter until soft and beat in the sugar until combined. Add the eggs, one at a time, beating well after each addition. Pour in the soaked fruit and orange zest and mix well. Sift in the flour and stir until combined. Spoon into the tin and bake for 3-3½ hours until cooked through.

Leave in the tin until cold, then wrap in greaseproof paper and foil and store in a cool place until needed.

Ideas for decorating the cake

•*A week before you plan to eat it, the cake can be covered with marzipan, left to dry out, then iced with royal icing.*

•*Arrange crystallized and glacé (candied) fruits and whole nuts in an attractive pattern on top of the cake, then brush them with a mixture of melted apricot jam or preserves and a couple of tablespoons of brandy or rum and leave the glaze to set.*

•*Decorate the iced cake with glazed winter fruits – kumquats and physalis – dipped in golden caramel. Put wide gold-wired ribbon around the cake.*

•*Thread fruit crisps or dried orange slices onto gold thread. Tie halved cinnamon sticks into bundles with gold thread and stack around the edge of the iced cake. Stand gold candles in the centre. Put wide gold wired ribbon around the cake.*

•*Put wired white ribbon decorated with gold stars around cake. Tie thread around bundles of gold-wrapped rectangular chocolates and place on the centre of cake and spilling over one side.*

•*Arrange marzipan holly leaves around the edges and toast lightly under the grill (broiler). Place alternate rows of glacé fruits and glazed nuts in the centre.*

•*Stud the cake with pecans or walnuts, then sprinkle with edible gold powder.*

Winter pudding

300ml/1¼ cups dry cider
225g /8 ounces prunes
115g/4 ounces dried apricots
115g/4 ounces brioche or Christmas pudding
150ml/⅝ cup milk
25g/¼ stick butter
115g/4 ounces sugar
Finely grated zest of 1 orange
3 tablespoons rum, brandy or whisky

Put the cider, prunes and apricots in a pan and bring to the boil, then reduce the heat and simmer gently for 10 minutes. Cover and leave to stand overnight.

Preheat the oven to 190°C/375°F/gas mark 5.

Butter a 1.1 litre/1 quart (approx.) baking dish. Reheat the fruit and cook, covered, until almost all the liquid is absorbed. Remove from the heat.

Crumble the brioche into the milk and allow to stand. Stir the remaining ingredients into the fruit until combined, then add the soaked brioche. Pour into the baking dish and bake for about 40-60 minutes until risen and cooked through.

Serve warm or cold with custard or cream.

You can use any dried fruits or a combination of fruits and nuts – as long as the total weight is 350g/12 ounces.

Candied fruit puddings

225g/8 ounces candied fruit, e.g. citrus peel, cherries, pineapple, etc.
3 tablespoon fruit liqueur (cherry, orange, etc.) or brandy
6 tablespoons caster (superfine) sugar
225g/8 ounces Madeira or pound cake, cut into 2.5cm/1-inch cubes
450ml/2 cups single (light) cream
4 eggs, beaten

Soak the fruits in the liqueur or brandy for at least an hour.

Preheat the oven to 180°C/350°F/gas mark 4.

Grease 6 dariole moulds (rum baba or timbale molds). Sprinkle 4
tablespoons of the sugar on the base and sides of the moulds.
Combine the soaked fruit with the cake cubes and divide among
the moulds.

Heat the cream and remaining sugar until the sugar has dissolved
completely. Remove from the heat, cool slightly then beat in the
eggs. Pour evenly into the moulds over the cake mixture.

Place the moulds in a large roasting tin (pan) and pour in hot
water to come halfway up the sides of the moulds. Bake for 40-45
minutes until the puddings have set. Remove from the water and
leave for a few minutes befo re turning out and serving with cream.

*These light little puddings are studded with candied fruits, which gives them a
jewelled appearance when turned out.*

Spiced fruit and wine tart

225g/8 ounces shortcrust (medium-flake) pastry
4 tablespoons sweet white wine
600ml/2½ cups double (heavy) cream
4 egg yolks
2-3 tablespoons sugar
Pinch ground mace
Pinch ground ginger
1 cinnamon stick
1 whole clove
1 teaspoon saffron threads
115g/4 ounces medjool dates, sliced
55g/2 ounces ready-to-eat prunes, sliced
55/2 ounces ready-to-eat figs, sliced

Preheat the oven to 220°C/425°F/gas mark 7.

Grease a deep 20cm/8-inch flan dish or pie dish. Line the dish with
the pastry and bake blind for 15 minutes.

Put the wine, cream, egg yolks, sugar and spices in a bowl over a
pan of simmering (not boiling) water and cook gently, stirring,
until starting to thicken. Leave to cool.

Reduce the oven temperature to 180°C/350°F/gas mark 4.
Put the dried fruits in the pastry case and strain over the cooled
custard. Bake for 20-25 minutes, or until the filling has set. Serve
warm or cold.

*This spicy fruit tart is made with sweet, plump medjool dates, which give it a
slight hint of toffee flavour.*

Chestnut tart

225g/8 ounces shortcrust (medium-flake) pastry
350g/12 ounces cooked chestnuts
1 tablespoon candied orange peel, chopped
50g/2 ounces sultanas (white raisins)
50g/2 ounces raisins
3 large eggs
150ml/⅝ cup double (heavy) cream
25g/1 ounce light muscovado (soft light brown) sugar
Finely grated zest 1 orange

Preheat the oven to 200°C/400°F/gas mark 6.

Roll out the pastry and line a 24cm/9½-inch flan tin or pie dish (or individual deep tartlet tins). Bake blind for 15 minutes. Remove the paper and baking beans and cook for another 10 minutes. Remove from the oven and reduce the heat to 180°C/350°F/gas mark 4.

Cut the chestnuts in half and combine with the candied peel, sultanas and raisins. Scatter evenly over pastry case. Whisk the eggs, cream, sugar and zest together and pour carefully over the fruit mixture. Cook for 30 minutes until set. Serve warm.

An interesting alternative to mince pies. You can make individual tarts instead of one large tart if you prefer.

Sherry butter biscuits (cookies)

200g/2 sticks butter
75g/3 ounces caster (superfine) sugar
3 tablespoons sweet sherry
375g/13 ounces plain (all-purpose) flour

Preheat the oven to 180°C/350°F/gas mark 4 . Grease a large baking tray.

Cream the butter and sugar until light. Gradually beat in the sherry, a little at a time. Add the flour gradually until the mixture forms a soft dough. Roll out the dough to 1.5cm/⅝-inch thick (try not to handle the dough too much or it will become greasy) on a lightly floured surface and cut into rounds.

Place on the baking tray and bake for 15–20 minutes. Cool on the tray (they will crisp as they cool) for a few minutes, then carefully transfer the biscuits (cookies) to a wire rack to finish cooling.

In the sixteenth and seventeenth centuries, a sweet wine was shipped from Jerez in southwest Spain. The name of the town was then spelled Xérès and pronounced 'sheris', and the wine was known as 'sherris sack'. Sack later became known as sherry and was a fashionable drink to serve in elegant eighteenth-century drawing rooms. Biscuits were also very popular at this time as stylish nibbles to accompany a glass of wine at social gatherings.

Wine sorbet

450g/1 pound caster (superfine) sugar
600ml/2½ cups water
300ml/1¼ cups sweet white wine, e.g. Sauternes
Juice of 2 lemons
Juice of 1 orange

Put the sugar, water and wine in a pan and heat gently until the sugar has dissolved. Bring to the boil and cook for 5 minutes.

Leave to cool for at least 1 hour and stir in the fruit juices. Pour into a freezer container and freeze until firm.

An elegant and sophisticated dessert that is definitely for adults only!

Wassail cup

1 litre/4½ cups ale or cider (applejack)
4 cloves
1 stick cinnamon, broken
2 teaspoons ground ginger
*50g/2 ounces light muscovado (soft light
brown) sugar*
150ml/⅝ cup water

Heat the ale or cider, spices, sugar and
water in a pan over a low heat until very
hot; but do not allow to boil. Strain into a
large bowl or heatproof glasses and serve hot.

*The practice of 'toasting' is thought to have been named after the pieces of
toast that were floated in the wassail bowl. This was a communal bowl filled
with hot spiced ale on which roasted apples and pieces of toast floated.
Everyone present drank from the wassail bowl as a sign of friendship.*

*Long ago throughout the British Isles, yule logs were blessed with wine by the
parish priest, and even the farm animals found ale or spirits mixed in with
their New Year feed. Priests also blessed wine and beer, and strong church
ales were sold in churchyards to welcome in the coming year. The custom has
survived to the present day, when glasses are filled as midnight strikes and a
toast is drunk for health and happiness in the year ahead.*

In some parts of the West Country on January 17, cider was poured around the roots of the oldest tree in the apple orchards, guns were fired through the branches to ward off evil spirits, and the youngest person present climbed up into the tree to place a piece of toast or cake soaked in cider in the branches while everyone sang the 'wassail song', asking the trees to bear large crops of juicy fruit for the coming year.

BURNS NIGHT

Scottish communities throughout the world remember the birth date of Scotland's best-loved poet, Robert Burns (born on January 25, 1759), with the traditional Burns Supper. Before the start of the meal, the 'Selkirk Grace' is recited; this is often wrongly attributed to Burns, but seems to have been in use as early as the seventeenth century.

> *Some hae meat and canna eat*
> *And some wad eat, that want it,*
> *But we hae meat and we can eat,*
> *And sae the Lord be thankit.*

The meal usually begins with cock-a-leekie soup, a tasty chicken soup that was a favourite of King James VI. A piper enters the room, followed by the chef carrying the haggis on a large plate. A waiter follows behind, carrying a bottle of whisky. They walk around the guests, ending up at the top table, where the chairman of the proceedings takes the whisky and pours out two large glasses. The piper is silent, the haggis is put on the table and the whiskies are given to the piper and chef. Then the haggis is 'addressed' by one of the guests from Burns's poem 'Address to a Haggis' (1786) with the lines:

> *Fair fa' your hones, sonsie face,*
> *Great chieftain o' the pudding-race.*

A dirk (dagger) is plunged dramatically into the haggis and a St Andrew's cross is cut on the top. The haggis is then served with the time-honoured accompaniments of 'bashed neeps' and 'champit tatties': mashed turnips and creamed potatoes.

After the meal, there are toasts of whisky to the Queen and 'the immortal memory' of Burns followed by other toasts. Everyone joins in the singing of Burns' songs, ending with 'Auld Lang Syne', followed by three rousing cheers for absent friends.

The first commemoration to celebrate the poet's life and works took place on the anniversary of his death on July 21 by a group of his friends. In the early 1800s, the first Burns clubs were set up, and Burns Night celebrations became the high point of their year. By 1885, there were over 50 clubs, and a central organization, The Burns Federation, was established. Nowadays Burns Night is held on the anniversary of the poet's birth, and is celebrated by Scottish communities throughout the world.

Burns Night may be a very formal event (as described above) or a more relaxed affair such as a simple supper with friends, but is certain to include haggis, a much-loved Scottish speciality. Haggis is possibly Scotland's most famous dish and is a mystery to most non-Scots. It is made from 'sheep's pluck' – the liver, heart and lungs – plus oatmeal, suet, herbs, spices and seasoning. Every butcher has his own secret recipe made according to the traditional basic recipe with the addition of other unique ingredients. A good haggis should be moist, firm and flavoursome.

Its origins are shrouded in mystery, although they are known to be ancient. Haggis or 'haggas pudding' was recorded in the early fifteenth century, and the name may come from the Scandinavian *hag*, the Anglo-Saxon *haecan*, the French *hachis*, or the Icelandic *hoggva*, meaning 'to hack or chop'. The earliest mention of haggis in Scotland seems to have been in the 'Flyting of Dunbar and Kennedy' (a series of satires) in 1508. Queen Victoria was very partial to haggis and enjoyed it when she stayed at Balmoral on Deeside.

Scotland is home to some of the finest foods in Britain, including many unique specialities still made according to original recipes and traditional methods.

Cock-a-leekie soup

1 x 1.3kg/3-pound chicken
1 bay leaf
2.25 litres/9½ cups stock or water
2 tablespoons whisky (optional)
1 teaspoon sugar
450g/1 pound leeks, sliced
1 onion, chopped
Salt and pepper
115g/4 ounces prunes (soaked overnight)
2 tablespoons rice

Put the chicken into a large
pan with the bay leaf and pour
in the water, whisky and sugar.
Cover and leave overnight.

Next day add the leeks, onion and salt and pepper to taste. Slowly
bring to the boil and simmer for about 2 hours or until the bird
is tender.

Skim off any fat from the liquid and remove the chicken from the
pan. Remove the skin and bones and cut the meat into pieces
before returning to the pan. Add the prunes and rice and simmer
gently for 15-20 minutes.

A favourite of kings James VI and I, this tasty soup is popular at Burns
suppers and could be called Scotland's national soup.

Rumbledethumps

450g/1 pound potatoes, thickly sliced
450g/1 pound white or spring cabbage, shredded
50g/½ stick butter
1 onion, finely chopped
125ml/generous ½ cup cream
Salt and pepper

Boil the potatoes and cabbage separately in as little water as
possible until cooked. Drain and mash the potatoes roughly.

In a large pan, melt the butter and add the onion. Cook gently for
5 minutes without browning, then add the potatoes and cabbage.
Stir in the cream and heat through, stirring until well mixed.
Season to taste and serve immediately.

The curious name of this dish comes from the meaning for 'bashed together',
i.e. 'rumbled and thumped'. It can be eaten alone as a vegetarian dish or
served with meat.

Scottish stuffed trout

6 trout, cleaned and gutted
50g/½ stick butter
3 onions, chopped
225g/8 ounces mushrooms
150ml/⅝ cup whisky
3 tablespoons chopped fresh herbs
Grated zest and juice of half a lemon
300ml/1¼ cups double (heavy) cream
50g/2 ounces wholemeal (whole-wheat) breadcrumbs

Preheat the oven to 180°C/350°F/gas mark 4. Grease a large
ovenproof dish or tin.

Put the trout into the dish or tin. Melt the butter and cook the
onions until soft. Add the mushrooms, 75ml/2½ ounces of the
whisky, the herbs and lemon zest and juice to the pan and simmer
for 5-10 minutes. Remove from the heat and stir in the cream and
the breadcrumbs. Cook gently over a very low heat until thick.
Divide the mixture evenly as a stuffing between the fish.

Pour over the fish and cook in the oven for about 30 minutes
until the trout is cooked through. Remove from the oven and
pour over the rest of the whisky. Serve immediately.

Trout is found in many Scottish waters and here is cooked in a whisky-
flavoured sauce.

Steak and whisky and peppercorns

25g/¼ stick butter
4 x 150g/5½-ounce fillet steaks
2 tablespoons whisky
175ml/¾ cup red wine
1 tablespoon green peppercorns

Melt the butter in a large frying pan and add the steaks. Cook for about 3-4 minutes on each side, depending on how well done you like your steak. Remove from the pan and keep warm.

Add the whisky to the pan and ignite carefully. Shake the pan until the flames subside, then add the wine and cook until it is reduced by a third. Add the peppercorns and stir until heated through. Spoon the sauce over the steaks and serve immediately.

Scotland produces superbly flavoursome, succulent beef. Perhaps the best-known is the famous Aberdeen Angus.

Haggis and beef whisky meatballs

450g/1 pound lean minced (ground) beef
375g/12 ounces haggis
1 egg
1 tablespoon malt whisky
Pinch of mace
Salt and pepper

Preheat the oven to 190° C/375°F/gas mark 5.

Combine all the ingredients in a large mixing bowl and blend with a fork until well mixed. Shape into balls and place on a baking tray. Cook for 20-30 minutes (depending on size) until cooked through.

These tasty meatballs use this uniquely Scottish speciality in an intriguing new way and are ideal for a buffet. They can be served hot or cold.

Howtowdie with whisky

<u>For the stuffing</u>
75g/3 ounces fresh breadcrumbs
3 tablespoons whisky
3 tablespoons cream
50g/½ stick butter, melted
1 small onion, chopped
1 tablespoon chopped fresh herbs
115g/4 ounces bacon or ham, diced
Salt and pepper

1× 2kg/4½-pound chicken (approx. weight)
75g/¾ stick butter
12 shallots
300ml/1¼ cups chicken stock
2 cloves
6 black peppercorns
1 blade mace (or ¼ tsp ground)

<u>For the sauce</u>
3 tablespoons whisky
3 tablespoons double (heavy) cream
25g/¼ stick butter

Preheat the oven to 200°C/400°F/gas mark 6.

Mix the breadcrumbs with the whisky, cream and butter until soaked. Add the rest of the stuffing ingredients, mixing well and place the mixture inside the chicken cavity.

Heat the butter in a large flameproof casserole and add the shallots, turning until lightly browned. Place the chicken in the casserole. Combine the chicken stock and spices and pour over the chicken. Cook in the oven for 20 minutes, then reduce the temperature to 190°C/375°F/gas mark 5, cover the casserole and cook for another 1½ hours or until the chicken is cooked through. Remove from the oven and keep the chicken warm.

Skim the fat off the juices and strain the juices into a pan. Add the whisky, cream and butter and heat gently until piping-hot, but do not allow to boil or the mixture will curdle and separate. Taste and add more whisky if you wish. Pour the sauce into a warm sauceboat or jug and serve with the chicken and shallots.

This is a variation of a seventeenth-century Scottish dish, the name of which may come from hutaudeau *(the Old French word for a pullet or young chicken), as the recipe has a definite French influence. The cooked bird was served on a 'nest' of spinach, surrounded by 'drappit' (poached) eggs.*

Pitcaithly bannock

225g/2¼ sticks unsalted butter
115g/4 ounces caster (superfine) sugar
350g/12 ounces plain (all-purpose) flour, sifted
50g/2 ounces blanched almonds, chopped
1 tablespoon caraway seeds, optional
25g/1 ounce candied peel, chopped

Preheat the oven to 150°C/300°F/gas mark 2. Lightly grease a baking tray.

Knead the butter and sugar together until smooth. Gradually work in the flour, almonds and caraway seeds until the mixture forms a soft dough. Shape into a thick round (the thickness is a matter of preference, but thicker will take longer to cook) and place on the baking tray. Press the candied peel into the top and bake for 30-60 minutes, or until cooked through

Carved wooden moulds are traditionally used for shaping Scottish shortbread. Lightly oil the mould with cooking oil and sprinkle with flour; shake off the excess flour and press the dough into the mould. Turn out onto a flat baking tray before baking.

Dundee cake

225g/2 sticks butter
225g/8 ounces caster (superfine) sugar
5 medium eggs
225g/8 ounces self-raising (self-rising) flour
½ teaspoon ground nutmeg
Finely grated zest of 1 orange
75g/3 ounces glacé cherries, rinsed, dried
  and quartered
175g/6 ounces currants
175g/6 ounces sultanas (white raisins)
50g/2 ounces candied peel, chopped
4 tablespoons milk
75g/3 ounces ground almonds
50g/2 ounces whole blanched almonds

Preheat the oven to 160°C/325°F/gas mark 3. Grease a 25cm/
10-inch round cake tin (pan).

Cream the butter and sugar until light and fluffy. Add the eggs, one at
a time, with a teaspoon of the flour, beating well after each addition.

Sift the remaining flour with the nutmeg and fold into the butter
mixture. Fold in the orange zest, fruits and peel and mix well.
Gently fold in the milk and ground almonds. Spoon into the tin
and slightly hollow the center with the back of a spoon. Bake for
1½ hours. Remove from the oven and arrange the whole almonds
on the top in circles. Return to the oven and cook for another
hour. Cool in the tin for 10 minutes, and then turn out onto a
wire rack to finish cooling.

It has been suggested that this famous cake it is a descendant of Dundee
gingerbread, or that the recipe was devised by the marmalade-makers as a
means of using up the surplus orange peel. To qualify as authentic, Dundee
cake should be lighter and more crumbly than traditional fruit cake.

Caledonian cream

3 tablespoons slightly bitter, chunky orange marmalade, such as Seville
2 tablespoons malt whisky
2 teaspoons lemon juice
300ml/1¼ cups double (heavy) cream
Sugar to taste
Candied orange peel or grated fresh orange zest to decorate

Whisk all the ingredients except the candied peel or grated zest until thick and smooth. Spoon into serving dishes and decorate with slivers of candied peel or sprinkle with orange zest.

Use a well-flavoured marmalade for this recipe, such as the slightly bitter Seville marmalade. The sweet 'jelly' type is not suitable. Caledonian cream is very rich but a little does go a long way; it's ideal for a special occasion, although not suitable for children or teetotallers.

Chocolate whisky truffle terrine

400g/14 ounces good-quality plain (dark) chocolate (minimum 70%
  cocoa solids)
200g/2 sticks unsalted butter
200g/7 ounces ground almonds
6 tablespoons malt whisky
2 tablespoons icing (confectioner's) sugar

Line a 1kg/2¼-pound loaf tin (pan) or 20cm/8-inch springform
round cake tin with cling film (plastic wrap).

Melt the chocolate with the butter over a low heat or in a
microwave oven. Remove from the heat and stir in the ground
almonds, whisky and sugar. Spoon into the lined tin.

Cover and chill overnight until completely set.

*Chocolate and whisky have a special affinity. This tempting dessert is very
rich, so serve small slices. It's particularly delicious with strawberries or
raspberries and/or cream or ice cream.*

Border tarts

225g/8 ounces shortcrust (medium-flake) pastry
55g/½ stick butter
115g/4 ounces raisins and sultanas (white raisins), mixed
1 egg
1-2 tablespoons whisky
115g/4 ounces light muscovado (soft light brown) sugar
25g/1 ounce walnuts, chopped

Preheat the oven to 190°C/375°F/gas mark 5.

Roll out the pastry and line small patty tins (pans) or a 20cm/ 8-inch flan tin or pie dish.

Melt the butter and stir in the rest of the ingredients, mixing well. Put a large teaspoonful of the mixture into each pastry case, or spoon the mixture into the large pastry case.

Bake for 15-20 minutes for the tarts and 30-40 minutes for the large tart. When cold, drizzle the top with icing if you wish.

Originally made with bread dough, this popular tart is nowadays made with pastry. The traditional filling adds whisky to make it even more irresistible!

Tablet

300ml/1¼ cups creamy milk
450g/1 pound sugar
115g/1 stick butter
Few drops vanilla essence

Place the milk and sugar in a heavy-based pan and heat gently until the sugar has melted, stirring constantly.

Bring to the boil and boil rapidly for about 20 minutes, until a little of the mixture forms a 'soft ball' when dropped into cold water. Remove from the heat and stir in the butter and essence. Beat until the butter has melted and the mixture begins to appear grainy.

Pour into a buttered tin and cut into squares when cold.

This sweet, sugary confection is an old Scottish speciality sweetmeat that's softer than toffee (taffy) but firmer than fudge. It's delicious served at the end of a meal with coffee.

Macaroon bars

1 heaped tablespoon mashed potatoes
450g/1 pound icing (confectioner's) sugar, sifted
225g/8 ounces plain (dark) or milk chocolate
Desiccated (shredded) coconut

Line a small square or rectangular tin (pan) with cling film (plastic wrap) or non-stick baking paper.

Work the potatoes with sufficient icing sugar to make a stiff mixture. Roll out on a surface dusted with icing sugar. Press into the prepared tin. Chill until firm and set.

Melt the chocolate in a bowl over a pan of simmering (not boiling) water or in a microwave oven. Sprinkle a thick layer of desiccated coconut onto a sheet of non-stick baking paper. Cut the potato fondant into bars and dip each into the melted chocolate, shaking off any excess. Place on the coconut-covered sheet to coat and sprinkle with more coconut. Leave to set.

This curious recipe produces a popular chocolate-covered fondant sweet that's sold throughout Scotland.

Index

almonds, liqueur frosted 265
angle cake 130
apples
    beer battered baked apples 74
    cider apple chicken with mushrooms 183
    roast pork with apples and pears 52
    toffee (caramel) 149
asparagus flan 70
Autumn 157–225

bacon
    cabbage and potato bake 38
    and egg salad 124
    with oysters 34
banana
    banana custard ice cream 136
    Scotch pancakes with bananas and
    toffee sauce 27
beer battered baked apples 74
bread
    boxty 41
    soda 40
boxty bread 41
buns, ravel 110
buttermilk
    Cumberland buttermilk cake 152
    scones 43

cabbage
    bacon and potato bake 39
cake
    angel 130
    carol singers' pepper cake 241
    chocolate banana loaf cake 59
    chocolate Easter nest cake 80
    cream custard cake 95
    Cumberland buttermilk cake 152
    fresh ginger gingerbread 203
    Irish Johnny cakes 44
    Irish porter cake 45
    Lancashire wakes cakes 142
    Mardi Gras king cake 29
    no-cook chcolate cake 61
    orange and spice dessert cake 57
    orange blossom cake 58
    rosemary and lemon sandwich cake 55
    strawbettery chocolage sponge gateau 129
    summer fruit cheesecake 112
    unbelievably rich chocolate cake 56

    Whitsun cake 111
Cambridge burnt cream tart 93
cheese
    and ale 91
    cutlets 89
    rich cheese fritters 88
    rich cheese tart 92
    Wensleydale pudding 90
cherry
    black cherry pancakes 20
    ice cream 155
    jubilee 153
    ripe flan 154
chicken
    cider apple chicken with mushrooms 183
    cold spiced 108
    and ham pie 120
    and mushroom pancakes 18
chocolate
    banana loaf cake 59
    chocolate nut pancake stack 21
    Easter nest cake 80
    fudge nut flan 76
    mousse 79
    no-cook chocolate cake 61
    punchtown 132
    strawberry chocolate sponge gateau 129
    unbelievably rich chocolate cake 56
    white chocolate rochers 62
clipping time pudding 127
coconut
    ice, uncooked 148
    macaroons 145
    pancakes 24
coffee
    Irish cream ice cream with Irish coffee
    sauce 47
cream
    Cambridge burnt cream tart 93
    Clotted cream ice cream 115
    cream custard cake 95
    Irish cream ice cream with Irish coffee
    sauce 47
    veal with cream sauce 50
crab 16
cucumber
    strawberry and cucumber salad 123
Cumberland buttermilk cake 152
custard, cream cake 95

duck with oranges 72

Easter 63
    chocolate Easter nest cake 80
egg
    bacon and, salad 124
    Scottish baked eggs 67

fadge 42
fairs, and wakes 138
figs, sugar baked 54
flan (see also tart)
    asparagus flan 70
    cherry ripe flan 154
floating islands 113
fortune telling crowdie 204
frittata, vegetable 105
fritter, rich cheese 88
fudge, creamy 151

geranium cream 98
ginger
    fresh ginger gingerbread 203
    ginger fairings 144
gooseberry
    fool 114
    and ice cream 99
    sauce 73
green salad with sherry-vinegar dressing
    125
gypsy tart 146

ham
    baked with cider and rosemary 107
    pie, chicken and 120
hasty pudding 94
honey syllabub 96
hummingbird cake 60

ice cream
    banana custard 136
    cherry 155
    clotted cream 115
    gooseberries and 99
    Irish cream with Irish coffee sauce 47
    raspberry ripple 134
    rum and raisin 261
    violet ice cream 78
iced punch tea 137
Irish cream ice cream with Irish coffee sauce
    47
Irish cream liqueur and butter pudding 46

Irish Johnny cakes 44
Irish porter cake 45
Irish stew with stout 38

Kentish pudding pie 75

lamb, roast with red wine gravy 71
Lancashire
    nuts 143
    wakes cakes 142
lemon
    rosemary and lemon sandwich cake 55
loaf, picnic 106
lobster 16

Mardi Gras king cake 29
May Day 84
Midsummer 117
Milk braised pork 87
Mothering Sunday (Mothers Day) 48
Mousse, chcolate 79
mushrooms 18
mussels 16

nougat 149
nuts
    chcolate fudge nut flan 76
    Lancashire 143
    peanut brittle 150

Oldbury tarts 109
orange
    duck with oranges 72
    orange blossom cake 58
    orange and spice dessert cake 57
oysters with bacon 34

pancakes
    basic 15
    black cherry with kirsch sauce 20
    chicken and mushroom 18
    chocolate nut stack 21
    coconut 24
    Gloucestershire suet pancakes 26
    potato flour 23
    Scotch, with bananas and toffee sauce 27
    seafood 16
    soufflé saucer 25
    St Clements 19
    Welsh 28
peaches, brandy spiced 133
peanut brittle 150

pears
    roast pork with apples and pears 52
peas
    cream of pea soup 122
picnic loaf 106
pies
    chicken and ham 120
pork
    milk braised 87
    roast pork with apples and pears 52
posset, sack 97
potato
    bacon and cabbage bake 39
    fadge 42
    glazed new 125
    potato flour pancakes 23
pudding
    clipping time pudding 127
    hasty pudding 94
    Irish cream liqueur and butter pudding 46
    Kentish pudding pie 75
    Spring herb 69
Punchstown chocolate 132

raspberry
    fool 131
    ripple ice cream 134
ravel buns 100
rosemary
    ham baked with cider and rosemary 107
    rosemary and lemon sandwich cake 55

sack posset 97
St Patricks Day 31
salad
    bacon and egg salad 124
    green, with sherry-vinegar dressing 125
    strawberry and cucumber salad 123
salmon
    sorrel, with 36
    spicy in pastry 103
    steaks with citrus and ginger 35
    tartare 104
sauce
    gooseberry sauce 73
    roast lamb with red wine gravy 71
    veal with cream sauce 50
    veal with wine sauce 51
Scottish baked eggs 67
scones
    buttermilk 43
Shrove Tuesday 12

spinach tart 77
Spring 6–81
    spring herb pudding 69
soda bread 40
soufflé saucer pancakes 25
soup
    cream of pea 122
    watercress 68
stew
    Irish with stout 38
stout, Irish stew with 38
strawberry
    chocolate sponge gateau 129
    and cucumber salad 123
    tarts 128
suet, Gloucestershire pancakes 26
Summer 83–155
summer fruit cheesecake 112
syllabub, honey 96

tarts (see also flans)
    Cambridge burnt cream tart 93
    gypsy tart 146
    Oldbury tarts 109
    rich cheese tart 92
    spinach tart 77
    strawberry 128
tea, iced punch 137
toad in the hole 171
toffee
    (caramel) apples 149
    Scotch pancakes with bananas and toffee
    sauce 27

veal
    with cream sauce 50
    with wine sauce 51
vegetable frittata 105
violet ice cream 78

wakes
    and fairs 138
    Lancashire wakes cakes 142
watercress soup 68
Welsh pancakes 28
Wensleydale pudding 90
Whit bank holiday 100
White pot 116
Whitsun cake 111
Winter 227–297